MODERN CUSTOM GUNS

Walnut, Steel, and Uncommon Artistry

Tom Turpin

Published by

 **krause
publications**

700 East State Street, Iola, WI 54990-0001

Please call or write for our free catalog. Our toll-free number to place an order or obtain a free catalog is
800-258-0929 or please use our regular business telephone 715-445-2214
for editorial comment and further information.

Library of Congress Catalog Number: 97-073035
ISBN: 0-87341-499-3
Printed in the United States of America

Some product names in the book are registered trademarks of their respective companies.
Coca-Cola™ • Cosmoline™ • Levi's™ • Teflon™

To Pauline Turpin
My best friend,
my hunting companion, and my wife

ACKNOWLEDGMENTS

Parts of this book have been previously published in a slightly different form in *GUNS*
Magazine. I express my deepest appreciation to Firearms Marketing
Group for permission to use some of the material again here.
I would also like to thank the gun makers and engravers and particularly the American Custom
Gunmakers Guild and the Firearms Engravers Guild of America
for their unwavering support in this project.
Finally, I express my admiration and thanks to my old friends Jim and Jackie Woods
who gave me encouragement when I needed it and for their helpful
suggestions in making the results of this effort a better book.

TABLE OF CONTENTS

The Old Timers
John Barraclough
Jim Blair
Erich Boessler
Winston Churchill
Mike Dubber
Bob Evans
William Gamradt
Eric Gold
Barry Lee Hands
Frank Hendricks
Ralph Ingle
Lynton McKenzie
Rex Pedersen
Marty Rabeno
Roger Sampson
Bruce Shaw
Ben Shostle
Ron Smith
Robert Swartley
Terry Theis
Lisa Tomlin
Terry Wallace
Sam Welch
Claus Willig

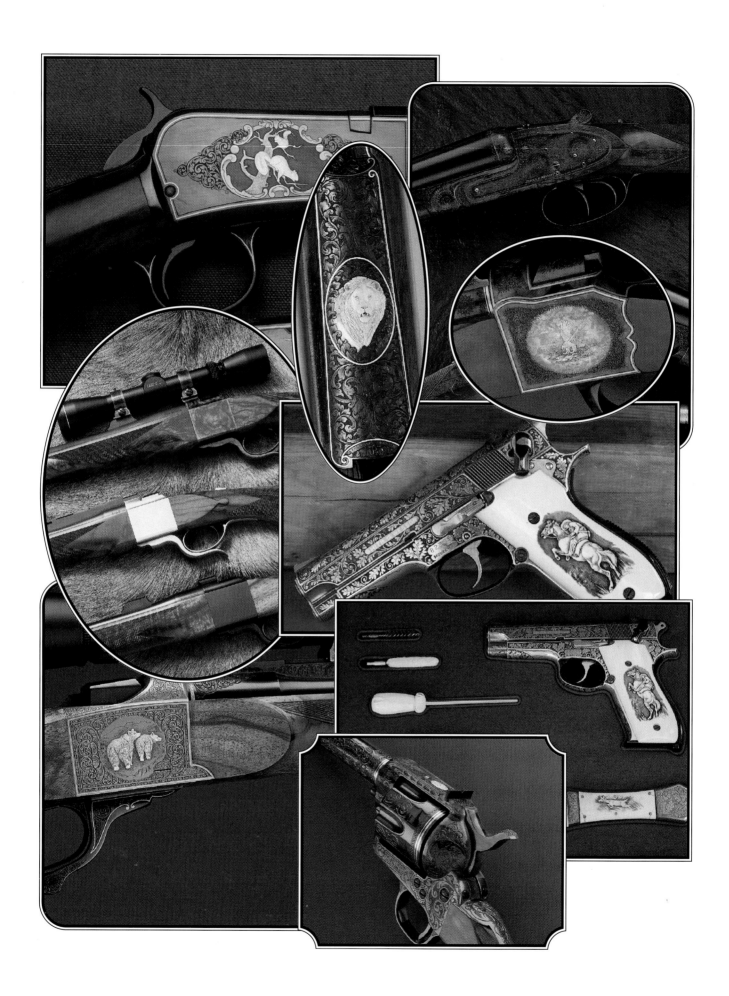

Introduction

Perhaps it was my early years that instilled a lifelong interest in custom guns in me. From my earliest memory, I knew about and appreciated custom gun work. A childhood pal of mine was mostly the cause. His grandfather, whom I never knew, had been a custom 'smith; he passed away long before I was born. Jimmy King was his grandson and we were like two peas in a pod. We spent all our waking hours together. Jimmy lived across the street from my grandmother where I spent most of my pre-school and summer vacation time. We played together at both his house and at my grandmother's.

Two of the author's custom rifles of a few years ago: left, a pre-64 Model 70 Winchester .338 with metalwork done in Germany and the stock by the late Jules LaBantchni, and right, also a pre-64 Winchester action rebarreled to 7x57 Mauser. The metalwork and stockwork was done in Germany.

Jimmy's father had stockpiled the old 'smith's tools in his garage where Jimmy and I often played. In addition, under the house, he had stored several thoroughly seasoned blanks of American black walnut left from the old man's stash. Although as memory serves me now, none of the blanks were fancy, they were as dry and seasoned as black walnut ever gets. Jimmy decided to restock his BB gun and the two of us reduced the blank supply to shavings. The 'smith's old drawknife—still sharp as a razor after years of idleness—was one of stored tools. That was my introduction to custom gunmaking.

In my early teens, a hunting pal of mine owned a locally produced custom rifle. Starting with a 98 Mauser action, the craftsman rebarreled it to a 30-06 and whittled out a stock from a stick of native grown black walnut. The rifle was fitted with a Balvar 8 scope from Bausch & Lomb. A rather odd scope by today's standards, it lacked internal adjustments. All the sighting adjustments had to be made in the scope mounts. It was a very good scope, but alas, has long since gone the way of the dodo bird. No doubt the lack of internal adjustments hastened its demise.

Many years later—when I was in college—a chum of mine and I decided to try our hand at stockmaking. We each purchased a 1903A3 Springfield from the Department of Civilian Marksmanship. We were able to arrange the purchase through the National Rifle Association. When we received them, the brand new rifles were still packed in Cosmoline. Next the two of us ordered a pair of black walnut stock blanks from Bishop, already roughly inletted and shaped for the Springfield. We removed the military stock and hardware from our Springfields and carefully fitted the Bishop blanks to the metal. We inletted and shaped our stocks using tools from the Industrial Arts Department of the college. Once we had sanded the stocks smooth, we finished them with a few coats of linseed oil. Actually, they didn't turn out too badly and we used our rifles proudly for such hunting as we were able to do at the time. Charlie Byrd, my gunmaking pal, was a

The Safari Club International Simba-M'Bogo rifle from the shop of custom maker Frank Wells. This rifle, along with all the accessories including the solid silver sculpture, sold at auction for $105,000. Photo by Ron Dehn, courtesy of Frank Wells.

much more proficient woodworker than I was. Consequently, his rifle was considerably more professional looking than mine.

One of our ROTC instructors, Sgt. Fowler, had served in Germany shortly after WWII. He showed me a rifle that a German gunsmith had built for him. It was, to my unrefined eyes, beautiful. Built on a military 98 Mauser action, it was still chambered for the 8x57 Mauser military cartridge. The maker had fashioned a new stock and fitted the rifle with a 4x European scope mounted in German claw mounts. He finished the rifle by doing a wonderful woodcarving job on the stock. Sgt. Fowler even let me shoot the gun a few times—it shot very well.

My first professionally built custom rifle was also made in Germany. I had somehow obtained another O3A3 Springfield, although I have long since forgotten the details of how I got it. I was serving a tour of duty with the US Army in Germany and was stationed at Panzer Kaserne, just outside the little town of Boeblingen. Fortunately, there was a gun shop with a resident gunsmith in the little town, and I dropped off my Springfield with him. With the rifle, I provided a Weaver K4 scope, a set of Redfield scope mounts, and a machine-turned black walnut stock blank. By this time, I was an avid Jack O'Connor reader and thanks to him, had developed some pretty firm ideas about custom rifle styl-

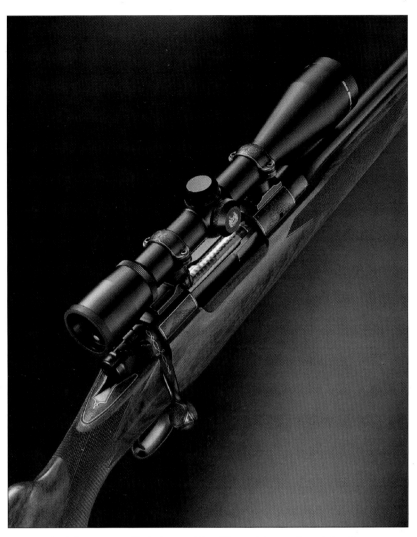

A wonderful custom rifle in 7mm-08 caliber with metalwork by Jim Wisner, stocked by Kent Bowerly, and engraved by Bob Evans. The action used appears to be a pre-64 Model 70 Winchester. Photo courtesy of the Firearms Engravers Guild of America.

ing. The gunsmith converted the parts into a nice sporting rifle in just a few short weeks. As I now recall, it cost me less than a hundred bucks for the job. The completed job was totally classic in styling, but still exhibited a few Germanic touches. He slimmed down the forend a bit more than I wanted and finished it off with a slight schnabel at the tip. Still, it was a pretty nice rifle and I was pleased with it.

Since that first rifle, I don't know how many custom guns have passed through my hands, but the number is substantial. Some were crafted in the shops of little known, but highly talented, artisans. Others were built by well-known makers who are often featured in the pages of the outdoor press. Many were built specifically for me, while others were made for someone else. Most of the work was superb, but some was not so hot.

I have often heard it said that craftsmanship is a dying art. The theory seems to be that as the older

legends in the business pass on, the younger generation isn't capable of doing the same quality work as did their predecessors. That is pure, unadulterated bunk! Some of the work turned out by mere youngsters is so good it's mind boggling. Frankly, much of the work done by custom makers of the past wasn't all that great when compared to that coming from the shops of today's artisans.

The best custom gunwork ever done in this country, or any other for that matter, is being accomplished today. I travel each year to a few national exhibitions, primarily Safari Club International's annual bash and the combined American Custom Gunmakers Guild/Firearms Engravers Guild of America Exhibition. Each time I return home thinking that I have seen it all, that no work is better, that perfection has been achieved, I am wrong. At the next exhibition, something is on display that is better! So it goes, year after year.

Perhaps, at some point in the future, a level of artistry in wood and metal will be reached that cannot be bettered. After all, perfection is perfection. Theoretically, one cannot improve upon that which is already perfect. Practically speaking, though, there is too much subjectivity involved ever to reach perfection. I doubt seriously if we could even define it acceptably, let alone achieve it. Perfection to one aficionado is barely satisfactory to another. As some wise sage once put it, "different strokes for different folks."

In this tome, the reader will be exposed to my idea of perfection in custom guns. It is opinionated throughout and full of thoughts on what I think a custom gun should be and by inference, should not be. Most of the photographs were chosen to illustrate my ideas of the superiority of the selected example. There are a few examples illustrated, though, that are not precisely my cup of tea. My objections to those few examples deal largely with styling and not craftsmanship.

A pal of mine recently took delivery of his newest custom rifle. He called me shortly after UPS delivered the latest creation and insisted that I come immediate-

ly to his place to have a look. I did, but out of friendship and not an agonizing desire to see his latest rifle. I've been through the experience many times before.

His taste in rifles and mine are at opposite ends of the spectrum. He absolutely loves glitter and flash in his rifles—exotic wood inlays, glossy finishes, rollover combs, fish scale checkering patterns, and gold inlaid maidens engraved with silver bath towels, cause my pal to swoon with delight. The same stuff gives me heartburn and apoplexy.

Looking at my rifles puts my amigo to sleep. They all have classic style stocks fashioned from good sticks of walnut. All feature satin oil finishes, are precisely checkered in either point or fleur-de-lis patterns, and all the metal surfaces are matte blued. Every time he has a bout with insomnia, a quick look at a few of my rifles cures his problem. If, on the other hand, I need to stay awake for a few days, a peek at his rifles will accomplish that for me. Even so, he loves his rifles as much as I love mine. His taste in rifles gives me chills and fever, but they are right for him.

That is one of the real advantages of the custom gun. All customers can get what they want in a firearm. My taste is conservative and muted. I want no glitter, no flash, no overt fanciness. There are hundreds of makers who are only too happy to take my order and deposit. My compadre, on the other hand, might have a bit more difficulty in finding a maker willing to satisfy his druthers. He can do so though, and has many times. We can both get what we want.

Three men have, most likely, had more to do with the development and success of the custom gun trade than all others combined and none of them were professional makers. All were members of the outdoor press who, in addition to their writing skills, were also

Not all custom rifles are traditional. Shown here are two rifles from Christensen Arms. On the left is a 22-250 Varmint model featuring a Remington 700 action, Pacific Research synthetic stock and a carbon fiber barrel. On the right is a Ruger 10-22 with laminated wood stock and again a carbon fiber barrel. Actually, the barrels are made up of a Shilen barrel liner, surrounded by a carbon fiber shell. Such barrels provide the stiffness of a heavy weight barrel without the weight.

The author's pet hunting rifle, an early David Miller custom .270 Winchester. This rifle has been around the world and has taken animals from the size of a 40 pound roe deer to an 1,800 pound Alaskan moose. Even with all the use, it will still shoot under .5 MOA any day of the week.

custom gun fans and users. One of the three did do a fair amount of custom gun work, and could probably be accurately categorized as a "semi-professional." The other two did no custom gun work that I am aware of. Two of the three have passed on to their heavenly reward (or ?????). The third of the trio is still going strong. I am referring to Jack O'Connor, John T. Amber, and Jim Carmichel. All three had a tremendous influence upon the trade like no others, before or since. O'Connor and Amber were contemporaries and Carmichel succeeded O'Connor as Shooting Editor of *Outdoor Life* magazine.

For those readers who have spent the last few years under a rock somewhere, Jack O'Connor was the Shooting Editor for *Outdoor Life* for more than thirty years. In addition to being an avid hunter and aficionado of custom guns, O'Connor was also a polished journalist. He was, for a number of years, the Professor of Journalism at the University of Arizona. He wrote numerous books on shooting, hunting, and firearms, as well as two novels and his autobiography—no telling how many magazine articles he wrote. He was also, in my opinion, the best of the lot. Born in 1902 in Tempe, Arizona, O'Connor came along at a time when game was more plentiful, game laws far more indulgent, and, after he tied his fortunes to *Outdoor Life*, the ability to hunt pretty much where and when he wanted.

Were it not for O'Connor, the .270 Winchester may have fallen by the wayside. Thanks to his publicizing his experiences with the cartridge, added to its performance in the hands of others, it is still, even in today's magnum mania atmosphere, one of the most popular cartridges of all time. The .270 Winchester cartridge and the name O'Connor will be inexorably linked together forever. To those who have read any of my prose, it is no secret that the .270 is also my favorite cartridge. My experience with the cartridge, although pale in comparison to O'Connor's, is directly comparable with his written assessments. He found the cartridge to be a very efficient killer and so have I. He noted that the 130 grain .277-inch bullet did not bounce off hair nor hide, and neither have I found

Four excellent rifles chambered for the .270 Winchester cartridge; three custom jobs, and a straight factory model. From left, a custom Heym SR-20 that was the prototype for the SR-20 Classic model, a Cecil Weems built, Shilen action, custom rifle, an early David Miller custom rifle, and a Remington Model 700 Light Mountain rifle. All are superbly accurate and a joy to hunt with.

This lovely custom rifle was put together by maker Jay McCament who did both the wood and metalwork. Engraver Bob Evans decorated the rifle with an unusual Aztec design engraving pattern. Photo by Mustafa Bilal, courtesy of FEGA.

11

that to be true. He found that a .270 bullet in the right place killed as well, and often better, than larger and more powerful cartridges. So have I.

O'Connor was also a lover of fine wood and precise checkering. Almost all of his personal battery of fire-

When discussing custom guns, rifles are generally the primary topic. There are many custom guns that are not rifles, though. This is the author's custom .45 auto, put together for target shooting. It is a tack-driver.

Start with a VHE grade Parker shotgun, and if you know the right craftsperson and are willing to spend the bucks it takes, you can end up with a "new" A1 Special grade gun. German engraver Erich Boessler did the metal upgrade and also the stock carving. The author did the rest.

arms were, at a minimum, custom stocked. Most of his stock jobs, at least from the mid-50s until his death, were done by one maker, Al Biesen. Over the years, he had several rifles built by other makers, but most were done by Biesen. Biesen stocked his first rifle for O'Connor in 1947, and the final one was not completed until after his death. As a matter of possible interest to O'Connor fans, the final rifle was a Ruger Model 77 chambered for the .280 Remington of all things.

Through his stories of hunting trips using rifles built by Biesen, Len Brownell, Earl Milliron, Al Linden, and many others, O'Connor directed the attention of his thousands of fans to the custom gun. Many makers in the business today owe their livings to Jack O'Connor.

One writer and editor whose influence on the custom gun trade was perhaps even greater than O'Connor's was his contemporary, John T. Amber. Amber was the Editor of *Gun Digest* for more than thirty years. He built that publication from little more than a pamphlet to the tome that it is today. I knew Amber well because he was my mentor in the writing business. He was rash, irascible, ornery, and downright cantankerous. He was also suave, debonair, charming, and a gentleman's gentleman. He knew guns like few of his peers. His two great loves in his life were single-shot rifles and custom guns.

Amber bought and published the second story I ever wrote for publication. My first was published in *Guns & Ammo* a few months earlier. Amber, though, saw something in me that he liked—don't ask me what it was, as to this day I don't know. Whether he felt that I had talent and would someday write well and knowledgeably, or whether he simply looked kindly upon me, I don't know. What I do know is that he took me under his wing and nurtured me along. He knew when to pat me on the back and give freely of his praise. He knew equally well when a size 10 boot, appropriately placed on my backside, was necessary. He was not reluctant to administer whichever motivational aid he felt was necessary.

The old man was a walking encyclopedia of firearms knowledge. Particularly fond of period single-shot rifles, he amassed a wonderful collection of outstanding specimens. So enamored was he with this type of rifle that he named his home base in Marengo, Illinois, Creedmore Farms. While he loved all fine firearms, it was the single-shot rifle that was his favorite.

Each issue of *Gun Digest* contained a lengthy pictori-

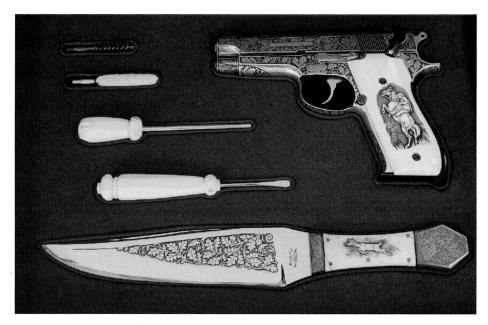

al section that showcased custom guns and custom engravings. In addition, it was a rare issue that didn't contain a feature article or two on the subject. Amber personally penned many of the articles, but he also avidly sought out other writers with expertise on the subject. In addition, he covered the European scene in the *Digest*, the only real source of data on European manufacturers and products from the American outdoor press. He attended and reported on most of the major European firearms exhibitions held each year, the lone member of the American press to do so. Amber was a trendsetter in many ways. He was also a wonderful man and a great friend.

Amber was instrumental in getting the American Custom Gunmakers Guild (ACGG) off the ground. He had a keen interest in the Guild and more appropriately, in the goals and intentions of its founders. He nurtured and cajoled a small group of artisans into forming the guild, and supported it strongly even after he drew his last breath. In his will, he bequeathed a substantial endowment to the guild to support the aims and aspirations of the organization for many years to come.

While both O'Connor and Amber kept custom guns constantly in the eyes of their shooting fans, they did so from two different perspectives. No doubt that both men loved fine custom guns—that is a given. I believe, however, that O'Connor loved them more so for their hunting use. He used his custom guns in the hunting fields all over the world. He wrote about them from the perspective of a hunter. Amber, on the other hand, wrote about custom guns from the perspective of the gun itself. Amber was a hunter, to be sure, but with nothing like the same level of passion as was the case with O'Connor. Simplistically stated, O'Connor used the custom gun to hunt. Amber hunted to use the custom gun. There is a major difference in

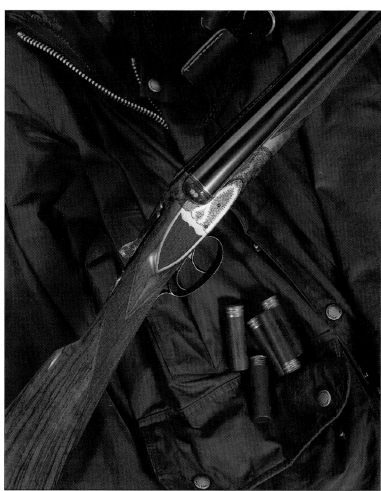

Steven Dodd Hughes specializes in unique projects. One of his specialties is building Hughes-Fox shotguns. He starts with an original Fox shotgun and completely rebuilds it, to include both metal and woodwork. This example of his work is nicely engraved by Eric Gold. Photo by Steven Dodd Hughes.

A Tom Volquartsen custom Ruger 10-22—although not normally thought of as a custom rifle, it really is by anyone's definition. Tom starts with a factory 10-22 action and replaces the barrel and stock, as well as several internal parts in the action. The resulting rifle is exceptionally accurate.

these two perspectives.

O'Connor finally "retired" from *Outdoor Life* when he learned that if he continued on the staff after a certain age, he would lose a substantial amount from his pension. He made a deal with his editor. He would retire, but continue to write for the magazine on a regular basis as a contributor. He would not be on salary, but rather on a fee-per-article basis. Apparently, the pact with the editor was a "gentlemen's agreement," sealed with a handshake. This worked nicely until the editor reached the mandatory retirement age as well. A new editor was named and the trouble started shortly thereafter. Finally, O'Connor could stand it no more and quit! He went to work for *Petersen's Hunting Magazine* and was still writing for it when he passed away.

O'Connor's replacement at *Outdoor Life* was a young Tennesseean. In addition to his talent as a writer, Jim Carmichel was both a home gunsmith and an avid competitive target shooter. O'Connor was neither. He apparently participated in few if any competitive matches or, at least, he never wrote about doing so. In matters technical, he was a real klutz. He often bragged that he didn't learn how to tie his shoes until half grown. Carmichel, on the other hand, is an accomplished competitive shooter and a talented amateur gunsmith. Naturally, he is also an avid hunter. He stepped in to fill a very large pair of shoes and has been doing so admirably for more than twenty years now.

Carmichel is also a lover of fine custom guns. In addition to his many magazine articles in *Outdoor Life*, he has authored several books. His book, *Jim Carmichel's Book of the Rifle*, is a standard reference on the subject. A sizable portion of that work is devoted to custom rifles and builders. He, like O'Connor and Amber before him, has helped along the careers of several custom

Two single-shot rifles, one from Dakota and the second from Heym, with substantial help from custom maker Bill Simmen: The Dakota Model 10 on the left features several optional features, most noticeably, special selection grade walnut for the stock. Bill Simmen custom stocked the rifle on the right, a Heym HR-38 Model.

The author's S&W Model 39 as modified by German Master Engraver Erich Boessler: Not only did Boessler do the wonderful engraving, but he also fashioned the elephant ivory grips and did the scrimshaw decoration.

A Bill Simmen-stocked Heym HR-38 chambered for the excellent 7x65R cartridge. The 7x65R is a rimmed twin of the .280 Remington.

makers who have come along since his predecessors left the scene. I first learned of guys like David Miller, Gary Goudy, and numerous others while reading Carmichel's prose.

A few other writers have boosted the lot of the custom gun craft—Col. Townsend Whelen, Elmer Keith, Pete Brown, and Warren Page from the past, and Craig Boddington, Ross Seyfried, Holt Bodinson, and perhaps another or two from the present. None have had

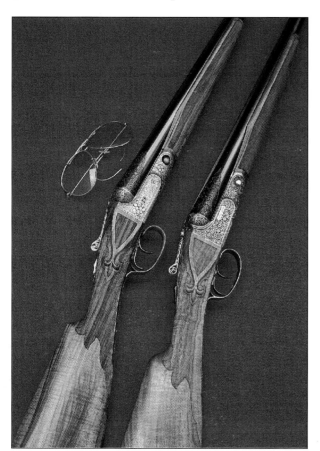

the impact of O'Connor, Amber, and Carmichel, though.

The title of this book refers to custom guns, but the reader will find that most of the material deals with custom rifles. I have made a valiant effort to cover both custom handguns and shotguns in the book. It is a fact, however, that most of the custom guns turned out today are rifles. As such, by necessity, the material in the book deals mostly with custom rifles. Early in the development process, considerable thought was given to restricting the book exclusively to custom rifles. We decided against that option primarily because there are custom shotguns and handguns that merit coverage in the book. To leave them out would be unfair to their creators.

With this short introduction to what is before you, sit back, relax, and enjoy. Stoke a favored pipe with your preferred concoction and pour a healthy portion of Scotland's finest dew before beginning. If you enjoy reading the prose only half as much as I enjoyed writing it, then we are both eminently successful.

Two lower grade Parker shotguns that have been upgraded to the A1 Special grade: The gun on the left features the late production-style engraving pattern, and the one on the right, the early production pattern. German Master Engraver Erich Boessler did the engraving and much of the metalwork.

Chapter 1

A Custom Gun— Why and Why Not?

Over the years, we have all read several "expert" definitions of what a custom gun is and, by inference, what it is not. Most of these definitions start by quoting from *Webster*. My copy of *Webster's New Collegiate Dictionary* defines custom as "made or performed according to personal order." It further defines custom built as "built to individual specifications." Neither definition is complicated nor difficult to understand. Unfortunately, arguments often follow because of this simplicity. The subject is far more subjective than objective, and personal opinion weighs heavily in any discussion of the subject. Some wise sage once said opinions are like behinds, everyone has one. Well, the sage didn't exactly use the word behind, but the point is the same. Some argue that unless the gun was built specifically for its owner, it is not a custom gun. If I accepted that definition, my pet custom rifle would not meet the criteria. The David Miller Company built my favorite custom job several years ago, although not for me. The client who had it built grew tired of rifles and took up competitive shotgun shooting. He swapped the rifle for a high grade shotgun. Miller learned of the trade and bought the rifle from the dealer. He gave it a thorough cleaning and general "spiffing up," then offered me the rifle.

Though the rifle is nothing like Miller's production at the time I obtained it, it was likewise nowhere near his prices at that time. It was still priced above my budget—anything would have been—but it was my only chance ever to own a David Miller rifle. I snapped it up. Since then, the rifle has been around the world with me. It has been frozen in Alaska and baked in Africa. It has been transported via Super Cubs, pack mules, gunbearers, and jumbo jets. Still, even after a jarring cross-country ride in a Landcruiser, it will put three shots under 1/2 inch.

Even though the rifle was not crafted specifically for me, it is still a custom rifle. There is but one and it is now mine. It would take a lot of bucks to get it away from me and even then I would have to be pretty hungry to part with it. It has served me so well that it is now in semi-retirement. I still drag it out once in awhile for a range visit or a short hunt. Usually, though, it occupies a place of honor in my gun cabinet.

There are many reasons to have a custom rifle built. Most are very valid, but alas, a few are not. My purpose in writing this chapter is to attempt to emphasize some of the many compelling justifications, and call into question some that may not be genuinely appropriate.

Most people are content with a tract home in a subdivision full of almost identical houses. Many of these houses are so alike that the occupant, particularly after an evening of swapping tall hunting tales and a "sundowner" or two, must be very careful not to wander into the wrong house! Others are not happy with anything less than an English Manor house on a 50 acre estate. Functionally, though, both houses provide the same thing: shelter, warmth, and, in one manner or the other, comfort.

A Volkswagen Beetle and a Rolls Royce Silver Shadow II each provide adequate transportation. Both cars, assuming normal maintenance and care, will reliably take the driver from point A to point B. The decision of which model to buy, however, has little to do with transportation. That choice is based more on taste, ego, and the size of one's bank account.

The debate is comparable to discussing a custom rifle versus the factory product. Both will satisfactorily do the job for which they were designed. Factory rifles vary in sophistication from the mass-produced Remington 700 and its competitors to the more refined Dakota 76 and similar rifles. They are excellent rifles. Each can be relied upon to deliver a bullet on the target, with groups measuring two minutes-of-angle (MOA) or less. For the hunter who uses a rifle merely as a tool, an assembly line model, identical to thousands of others, is usually plenty good enough.

On the other hand, for those who want only the best, or who appreciate beauty and admire technical virtuosity above all else, a full custom job is the only way to go. Not only can these aficionados have their rifles built to fit them exactly, but they also may specify wood, finish, checkering pattern, accessories, and, if wanted, engraving. They can, if they are of a mind to do so, develop a unique cartridge and have a rifle wrapped around it. They can have precisely what they want and can rest assured that the finished rifle will be the best in the world. There is no question that the finest rifles on the globe are crafted by our custom artisans here in the United States. No one else even comes close.

There is one aspect of rifles, whether factory or custom, that needs an honest discussion—the frequently maniacal concern for accuracy. Judging from my more than forty years of personal experience and from what I have read during the same period, there is apparently a dichotomy between what is written about accuracy and what I have experienced at the range. Either most writers on the subject are much better shooters than I am, or they have been far luckier in obtaining super accurate rifles. I won't say that perhaps some did most of their shooting with a typewriter!

In my rack, I have a half dozen or so superbly accurate rifles. Most are custom jobs, or at least have been customized in one fashion or another. Yet, that fact doesn't mean that they are superbly accurate *because* they are custom jobs. It just so happens that *all* my personal rifles have at least some custom features. Had I used only factory rifles during the same period, I'm

sure that I would have approximately the same number of tack-drivers.

Long ago I lost count of just how many rifles I have owned over the years. I would guess at least a couple hundred have gone through my hands. Most of them were taken to the range for a trial. If a rifle would group MOA or less, it went into my keeper rack. If truly accurate rifles were as common as one would believe from reading all the published hype, my tack-driver rack should contain many more rifles than it does. From my experience, I believe that MOA capable rifles are far less commonly encountered than popular opinion or media hype seems to suggest.

Frankly, I think too much importance is attached to it anyway. Unless the shooter is into the benchrest game or an avid varmint shooter, MOA or better accuracy is not obligatory for a perfectly satisfactory hunting rifle. Lest there be a misunderstanding, let me make it clear that I advocate trying to get every bit of

Starting with a Dakota left-hand action, custom maker Jay McCament crafted this exquisite rifle chambered for the .280 Remington cartridge. Stocked to the muzzle in French walnut, the rifle weighs but 7-1/4 pounds and features an octagon barrel. McCament did both the metal and stockwork. Bob Evans did the southwestern theme engraving. Photo by Mustafa Bilal.

A favorite turn-of-the-century target rifle, the Stevens 44-1/2 is making a comeback with the modern CPA action. This example was barreled and chambered to shoot a breech-seated bullet in .32-40 caliber using a single cartridge case. Both the rifle and the photo are by Steven Dodd Hughes.

accuracy from a rifle that is humanly possible to obtain. Many can be improved, often profoundly, by tinkering with the bedding, playing with the screw torque, and carefully developing a load that works best in a given rifle. When all that has been done, though, and still the best groups that can be obtained are 1.5 to 2 MOA, no big deal. Such accuracy is satisfactory for a hunting rifle, despite the malarkey to the contrary. The biggest variable in the accuracy game has little to do with the rifle anyway. The most significant inconsistency is the shooter.

We all know people who, even when shooting a rifle that delivers .5 MOA groups, still can't hit Elmer Keith's hat at 100 yards. Others, using a rifle that is not particularly accurate in the hands of most shooters, can blast the wings off a gnat! No rifle builder can alter this fact, no matter how talented the individual maker might be. This is a reality that must simply be accepted. Naturally, this truth can cause problems

between the maker or manufacturer of a rifle and the shooter. It's pretty tough to tell someone that the problem isn't the rifle, but instead is his or her ineptitude at the range. Most cannot accept the fact that the sling-shot-sized groups they've been getting are caused by flinching, jerking, poor vision, or, for whatever reason, that they just can't shoot accurately.

I've known men who ordered custom rifles singularly because they couldn't shoot better than dinner plate-sized groups with factory models. Apparently, they think that a custom rifle will cure their shooting woes. I recognize that the average custom rifle is generally more accurate than the average factory product. Most quality makers go to extraordinary lengths to true all the surfaces of the action, insure that the bolt is concentric with the bore, and hone the trigger to permit a safe, but effortless release. They will scrape for hours and remove almost microscopic-sized shavings of wood from the stock inletting to obtain a near perfect mating of wood and metal. All this precise work contributes greatly to the accuracy potential of a rifle.

Still, one of the most consistently accurate rifles I have ever owned is a factory model. Well, that is not totally factual. More correctly stated, it is mostly a factory job. The rifle is a Remington Model 700 Light Mountain Rifle in .270 Winchester caliber. I borrowed the rifle from Remington for a story I was doing on the .270. When I received it from the factory, the stock had a hairline crack above the grip, probably because it was transported under a piano. Fortunately, the crack was minor and did not appreciably weaken the stock. I mounted a scope on the rifle and took it to the range. It was superbly accurate in spite of the cracked stock. It was so accurate and lightweight that I decided to make a deal with Remington to keep it.

When I had finished the .270 story, I removed the defective stock and sent the barreled action to Mark Phipps, President of Garrett Accur-Light, Inc., Fort Collins, Colorado. Phipps custom-bedded the factory metal into one of his Ultra-Light synthetic stocks. The finished rifle, complete with scope Leupold 2x7 variable, weighs but 7-1/4 pounds. Even so, it will shoot .5 MOA groups any day of the week. The metal is untouched and remains just as it came from Remington.

Precisely why one rifle is superbly accurate and another, an apparently identical one, scatters its shots with all the precision of a ten dollar BB gun, is not known with certainty. I suspect that we know far more about the reasons for inaccuracy than we do the reverse, the causes of accuracy. This notion makes sense to me. If we really knew the answers, all rifles would be splendidly accurate.

There is no doubt that the major contributor to accuracy is the barrel. No matter how precisely a rifle is put together, if the barrel has flaws, it simply won't shoot. Obviously, a good barrel can be made to shoot poorly by slipshod work. I do not believe, though, that a problem barrel can be made to shoot accurately, no matter what.

Unfortunately, there is only one way to figure out whether a given barrel will shoot precisely. It has to be threaded and chambered, fitted to an action, bedded into a stock, and taken to the range and shot. It would be wonderful if we had something similar to an electrical voltmeter that could be connected to a barrel for an accuracy reading, but alas, technology has not yet come up with such an indicator. Until someone invents such a device, shooting is the only way to decide the accuracy potential of a barrel.

Another reason often provided for ordering a custom rifle is to obtain better functioning. Here again, I submit that the average custom rifle will function better and certainly smoother than its factory counterpart, but I don't think the functional difference is substantial enough to justify ordering a custom job for this reason alone. Most custom 'smiths spend many hours honing the action for their creations until they eliminate all roughness. Many will even machine a new follower specifically for the caliber of the rifle. Rails will be ground and polished as necessary. When they are finished, the resulting rifle will function flawlessly. In all fairness, though, I must say that most of the factory products function well. They might not have the ball-bearing smoothness of a custom job, nor should it be expected. To get the Teflon smoothness of most custom rifles requires many hours of skilled hand work and that translates into money. For the $500 price of a new factory product, give or take a few bucks, you simply aren't going to get it. Error free function yes, but hot-knife-through-butter smoothness just isn't in the cards. As some wise sage once said, you can't make a silk purse out of a sow's ear!

Factory rifles can be compared to the VW Beetle or the tract home. Economical and dependable, they will do the job for which they were designed and will do it well. Don't expect bells and whistles, though. For the price of a Beetle or a sub-division model, expect only the necessities. If bare necessities are not enough, then it is time to start looking toward the Rolls or the palatial estate, or somewhere between the extremes.

I believe that custom rifle accuracy and function are insufficiently superior to a factory model to justify investing in one for either reason. Having said that,

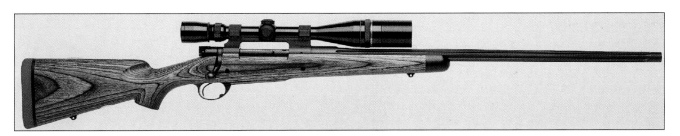

An example of a long-range hunting rifle from the David Miller Co.: As an avid trophy Coues deer hunter, Miller learned early on that the monster bucks he sought didn't reach the required age and maturity by being dumb! They stayed out of range. He designed and made the Marksman Model to even the odds. Photo by Ron Dehn.

however, if individuals want a custom rifle for whatever reason, they should arrange with a maker to have one built. The only necessary reason is that they want one. That is justification enough. All I am saying is that if the customer demands that a custom rifle shoot better than any factory rifle, he or she may be disappointed. That can lead to unfair and unnecessary conflict between the builder and the client.

A very precise and fastidious custom shop is the David Miller Company in Tucson, Arizona. David Miller and his associate Curt Crum build resplendent rifles. I have watched them work for hours on end and I can confirm that none are more conscientious, meticulous, or painstaking in their craft. They will spend hours on a detail that most connoisseurs would consider minor. Even so, the David Miller Company *only* guarantees its rifles to group 1.5 MOA. Admittedly, many, if not most, will shoot better than that. Still, there is no assurance of better than 1.5 MOA accuracy. I know of few makers that will certify their rifles to shoot better than that.

Another reason for not having a custom gun built is, like the others, a bit controversial. A few of my friends have had numerous custom jobs done for investment purposes. Presumably, they expect that with the passage of time, the value of the guns will increase. Frankly, I think they are just using that premise to justify ordering another custom gun to their wives. The fact is, though, that unless one is really lucky, custom guns are not good investments. Logically assessed, it only makes good common sense why this is so.

Why would anyone pay the replacement cost or even more, for someone else's custom gun? For the same amount, they could have one built for themselves. I make a practice of attending most of the gun shows in the local area. One old fellow had a table full of custom rifles at every show I attended for several years. The rifles were very nice, although none were crafted by well-known makers. Still, each and every one was a high quality piece. The prices he was asking for the rifles were more than reasonable—they were really quite cheap. Not one that I saw could be replaced for anywhere near his asking prices. Most were priced at about the cost of an action, barrel, and stock blank.

Even so, I saw the same rifles on his table at show after show. I suppose he sold an odd one every now and then, but mostly, when the show was over, he took them back home. He had his table at the last show I attended, still full of rifles. Now, I'm sure that had he displayed pieces from Dave Miller, John Bolliger, Steve Heilmann, or any one of several others at those prices, they would have been gone in a heartbeat. Of course, he would have lost ten times what he was losing on the pieces he was trying to sell. That, to me at least, is not a very good investment.

If great improvements in accuracy and function are not valid reasons for having a custom job done, and in this scribe's opinion they aren't, what, then, are the cogent reasons? I can say with confidence that there are far more reasons to have such a rifle built than not.

As I mentioned earlier, the primary reason for placing an order for a custom rifle is that the buyer wants one. That is an unarguable motivator and the primary justification for most of my personal custom rifles. The only nondebatable argument not to have one built is the cost. Sadly, all cannot afford to have a rifle built to their specifications. Impeccable, meticulous work doesn't come cheaply. Personally speaking, I would have far more custom rifles in my rack than are there if only I could afford more.

What, then, are the reasons, other than want, to put a deposit down with a builder and sign on the dotted line? One is fit. Factories design their rifles to fit the mythical "average" person. Things such as length of pull, drop at the heel and comb, length of forearm, cast on or cast off, and the like are standardized to fit the average Joe. I don't know how the manufacturers arrive at their standard dimensions, but they do a masterful job of it. Most out-of-the-box factory rifles match my personal requirements pretty well. Physically, I must coincide with the average mold. I'm 6 feet-2 inches tall, weigh about 200

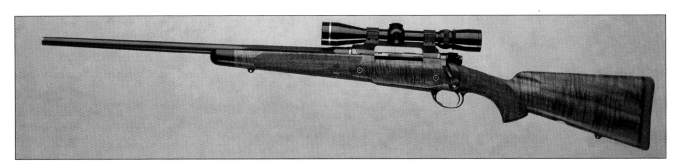

This exquisite custom rifle is from the David Miller Co. Long recognized as one of the very best makers in the country, the team of David Miller and Curt Crum leave nothing to chance when they build a rifle. Even the scope mounting system is custom built in the Miller shop. Photo by Ron Dehn.

A John Bolliger Signature Series Custom rifle chambered for the .416 Remington magnum cartridge. Bolliger's Mountain Riflery in Pocatello, Idaho, did all the work except the engraving. That task was turned over to Lisa Tomlin. Photo courtesy of John Bolliger.

pounds, and wear a 33-inch sleeve length. I do not feel handicapped using the standard dimensions of a factory rifle. Most people are pretty adaptable in conforming to any situation. Yet, for a woman, a uniquely short or tall person, someone who is physically handicapped in some way, or has "atypical" physical dimensions, a standard factory rifle might not work very well. Most make do with it anyway. After all, most field situations allow sufficient time to struggle with a rifle that really doesn't fit. An ill-fitting shotgun in the field is another matter, but standard rifle dimensions work pretty well for most users.

How we learn to shoot also makes a big difference. For example, most European-made rifles have longer stocks, i.e., length-of-pull, than American made rifles do. I worked as a consultant to a major German rifle manufacturer for some fifteen years. Its standard factory dimension for length-of-pull is 14-1/2 inches, whereas the US standard is about an inch less. Try as I may, I could never get the company to change it. It simply couldn't understand—or wouldn't accept—that its stocks were too long for the average American shooter. The reason was simple: European shooters

are taught to shoot with their heads erect on the stock and American shooters, on the other hand, tend to "crawl" the stock with their cheeks firmly welded against the comb of the stock. That is also the reason, by the way, why normal European scope mounts are considerably higher than American mounts. As far as I know, the German company is still merrily turning out stocks considerably too long for most American shooters.

To get a rifle that really fits, the custom route is the only way to go. The selected maker will measure a client precisely and custom craft a rifle to exactly fit the need. No longer will the rifle butt catch under their armpit when shooting a rifle that is too long. At the other extreme, neither will they bash their noses or lips with their thumbs when it is too short. Lo and behold, when they shoulder their rifles, they won't have to manipulate their heads to bring their eyes in exact line with the scope. It will be there—automatically. Then and only then can the shooter concentrate on the target to the exclusion of everything else. That is the beauty of using a rifle that fits, rather than adapting to one that doesn't.

An example of a custom rifle that turned into a factory production model: The Heym SR-20 Classic rifle model was spawned from the author's custom .270 Winchester that was built around the Heym action. No longer imported into the US, the SR-20 Classic was a fine factory rifle.

Another reason for having a custom rifle built is to get one chambered for a caliber that isn't available in the factory products. Many, mostly advanced shooters, delight in cartridge development. They do so with all the fervor of Edison working on his light bulb. Even so, I can't think of a gap in the readily available calibers on the market. Whether the quarry is a cottontail rabbit or a Jurassic Park dinosaur, perfectly suitable and effective calibers are available over the counter from the various factories. Still, if a given shooter has developed a .30 Super Wazoo Maxi-Mag and wants a rifle chambered for it, why not! Someone once said, variety is the spice of life, and although I don't think the speaker was referring to rifle calibers when making the statement, it does apply.

I have several friends who constantly work with rifles and loads and try to come up with a magical caliber that will lay everything low at the mere mention of the name. Others do so just to have their names on a caliber. Their creations, though a ballistic clone of a half dozen readily available cartridges, are quickly dubbed the .396 John Doe Pooper Scooper or some such moniker. Claims of velocities approaching the speed of light are commonplace around the camp-fire. If such balderdash makes them happy, why not.

Of course, this brainchild won't kill an animal any quicker or deader than the ancient 30-06 or .270, but this fact doesn't enter the equation. That is what they want, and as long as they can afford to have one built and can find a maker to build it, more power to them. Listening to claims of the superiority of their development sometimes gives me a case of hives, but what the hell!

The major reason for having a custom rifle built, though, is not only to have a tool for hunting, but also to have an example of exquisite craftsmanship to be appreciated. A rifle, any rifle, spends far more time in the rack than it does in the field. Likewise, an average hunter spends far more time in the den than in hunting camp. A fine custom rifle is something that can be admired, night after night, and shown off to a few friends when swapping tall tales of daring-do. Somehow, a paneled den, a few sundowners, and a custom rifle just seem to go together. The glow of hand-rubbed walnut, precise checkering, and flawless execution fit the mood. The mirror finish on a factory product would be out of place, not unlike a hooker in work clothes showing up at a church social.

I have a friend who has a wonderful collection of custom rifles. I don't think any of his custom rifles

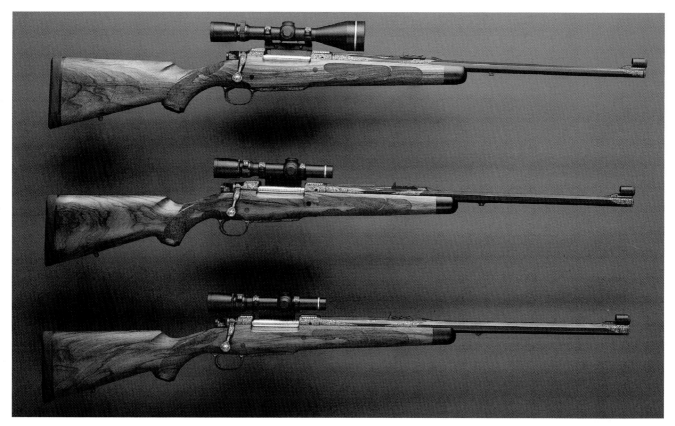

A closely matched trio of fine custom rifles from the Tucson shop of Frank Wells. Wells started with three BBK-02 actions and three closely matched blanks of English walnut. All metal and stockwork was done in his shop. The rifles are chambered for the .340, .416, and .460 Weatherby cartridges. The matching engraving patterns are the work of Ken Warren. Photo by Ron Dehn.

have ever been in hunting camp. Instead, his hunting rifle is a synthetic-stocked factory model. He is a collector of fine custom rifles, but not a user. There is absolutely nothing wrong with that, although I couldn't personally do it. I'm convinced that even if he could be persuaded to take one of his custom rifles to the field, he wouldn't enjoy the hunt. He would be far too busy worrying about putting a ding or a scratch on one of his creations to relish the experience. Contrast that to another pal who has but one custom rifle, a .375 H&H. When he treks off to Africa on another safari, he takes but the one rifle. After several such trips, the rifle has accumulated a few honest scars. There is no way this pal would have the scars repaired. To him, they are marks of honor for the rifle.

I am a great admirer of custom guns in general and custom rifles in particular. I delight in showing my friends the results of many hours of highly skilled labor by various extremely talented makers. I take great pride in the collection of custom rifles that has taken me a lifetime to obtain. Yet, my custom rifles were made to use, and not simply sit in the rack to be admired.

As mentioned earlier, my pet of pets is a rifle that was not even built for me. The original owner must have been exactly my size, though, because the rifle

fits me like a glove. It is chambered for the .270 Winchester cartridge, my favorite caliber. I was busier than Wimpy at a table full of hamburgers as I prepared to leave on a combination moose and caribou hunt in Alaska when David Miller called about the rifle.

Miller's shop is in Tucson, about 75 miles from my home in southeastern Arizona. With my departure for the hunt barely two weeks off, I just didn't have enough time to drive to Tucson to see the rifle. Miller gave up some of his shop time and brought it to me. The rifle was in pristine condition, although it had a few dings here and there from handling. It had obviously been used very little. We made a deal and he took the rifle back to his shop to clean it up for me. Three days before my departure, I took the rifle to the range and got it properly sighted. My first three-shot group with it measured just .740-inch, which is remarkably accurate by anyone's definition.

I simply had to take it with me on the hunt, although I concede that the .270, as good as it is, is not an ideal moose caliber. It is fine for caribou, but pretty light for a 1,500 pound plus moose. Even so, I had previously lived in Alaska and subsisted on moose meat for a couple years. I knew that, for such a large animal, a moose has a glass jaw. A properly placed bullet of just about any caliber will cleanly take a moose. I took the rifle with me and ten days later, I had my moose and caribou in the meat locker.

A year later, I had the same rifle with me on a combined mule deer and antelope hunt in Wyoming. The camp was located on Savery Creek, not far from Baggs, close to the Colorado border. Savery Creek country is, to this Arizonan anyway, a rather odd combination. It consists of somewhat flat country down where the creek flows, and merges into very steep and rugged hillsides, which rises several hundred feet from the valley floor. Once on top, however, it evens out into billiard table flat sage brush country. It was during this hunt that I made the longest two shots on game that I have ever attempted.

I am not a believer in long shots at game. I learned long ago that long shots generally result from laziness or poor hunting techniques. It is pretty unusual that the hunter cannot get to within a reasonable shooting range of an animal. In addition to that, if in fact it is impossible to get closer, taking a chance on an exceptionally long shot is rarely justified. Unless the animal is really exceptional, the shot should be passed. Blazing away at 105mm howitzer ranges usually results in either wasted ammo, or, far worse, a wounded animal.

Anyway, my guide and I were up on top well before daylight. From our vantage point overlooking an area where the guide had seen many good bucks, we awaited the new day. As it became light enough to see, nothing was within view. On a distant hillside, though, perhaps three miles off, we could barely make out a couple of deer. From that distance, we couldn't tell if the deer were bucks or does, but we thought it would be worth hiking over for a look. We left our vantage point and started working our way in the direction of the deer when the guide froze up like a setter on point. There in the sage flats, were two bucks staring directly at us. One looked to be a monster.

He whispered to me that the one buck was super, but had already spotted us. There was no way in the flat sage to get any closer. If we were going to try for him, it would have to be from where we were. When he said that, I looked at him as though he had three heads! To me, the buck appeared to be at least 800 yards away, and I said so. The guide said no, that it was closer to 500. He informed me that the early morning light there was very tricky which made accurate range estimation very difficult. I didn't tell him that I had trouble estimating range on a well marked football field! Anyway, he felt the buck was good enough to justify such a long shot.

As luck would have it, there was a fence row within 20 feet of us, so I eased over to a post and took a rest. It was almost as solid as a concrete shooting bench. I lined the horizontal crosswire on the top of the buck's antlers, and the vertical wire on his shoulder. At the shot, the buck didn't move. Standing in the sage brush as he was, I knew the shot was high. Had it been too low, we would have seen the bullet strike the sage. I lowered the horizontal wire to the top of the buck's head and the second shot killed the buck in his tracks. He went down so fast that we had a heck of a time finding him in the sage.

As it turned out, we paced the distance to the buck and found that he was a little over 400 yards, not 500 or 800. In addition, he was not nearly as huge as we had thought. He had really fooled us terribly. Knowing my rifle and its ballistics enabled me to make the shot, but poor range judgment almost caused me to blow it. As a result of this experience, less than twenty-four hours later, I dropped a big buck antelope under almost identical circumstances, except

A beautiful custom Model 70 Winchester from the shop of stockmaker Keith Heppler. Chambered for the .270 Winchester, Jack O'Connor would have been proud to own this classic custom rifle. The metalwork was executed by Heppler's brother Larry and Richard Bouchet did the beautiful engraving. Photo by Mustafa Bilal.

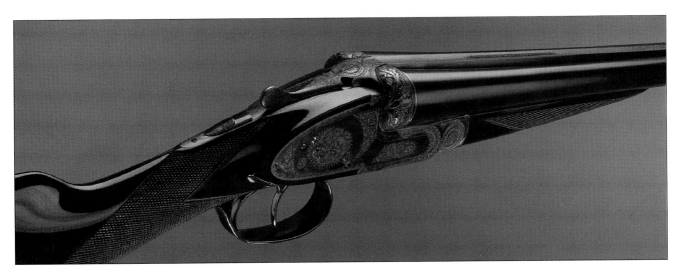

One of a cased set of guns from the shop of Steve Heilmann, this double looks decidedly English. Surprisingly, it was originally made in France in the 1890s. Heilmann refurbished the gun into new condition and Terry Wallace did the marvelous engraving. The other gun in the set by the same artisans is a .375 H&H magazine rifle. Photo by Rick Waller.

he was 100 paces further away!

Since these hunts, the rifle has been with me around the world. With it, among other animals, I have taken kudu, impala, bushbuck, and warthog in Africa, several antelope and mule deer in Wyoming and Montana, and roe deer, chamois, and red deer in Germany. When I returned from my last African safari, I took the rifle to the range to check the zero. Even after riding several thousand miles in various airplane cargo bays and being loaded and unloaded by numerous ham-fisted baggage handlers who could break an anvil, the first three-shot group measured .263 inch. This is the smallest group that I have ever shot with any rifle.

The rifle is now in semi-retirement. It has paid its dues many times over. I have often considered sending the rifle back to Miller to restore it back to its original pristine condition. It would take very little to do that—a little touch-up on the checkering, another coat or two of finish on the stock, and perhaps a new blue job. Yet, each time I get this thought, I look at the honest scars of use, not abuse. Each scar has a story and a memory. I think I will let it be.

This is the joy of owning and using custom rifles for me, and I don't think I am all that different from most enthusiasts. I suspect than most orders for a custom job are based upon similar persuasions. I can't imagine having comparable feelings for a factory rifle.

There you have it, one person's opinion of how to justify a new custom rifle and what not to use as an excuse. As I see it, there are three somewhat valid grounds for not ordering a custom rifle. First, and most obvious, is that such a rifle is unaffordable. Second, a custom rifle shouldn't be ordered to overcome poor shooting. No custom rifle, no matter how

well done, can do that. Third, a custom rifle will not generally function any more positively than a factory product. Smoother and slicker yes, but both should function error free.

The reasons for plunking down a deposit on a custom job, though, are many. The rifle styling, while representative of the selected builder's work, is also a reflection of the buyer. The choice reveals the buyer's taste, or lack thereof. The choice in rifles says much about one's general personality. The person whose taste in rifles runs to what I like to call quiet elegance, generally prefers subdued refinement in all other aspects of his or her life. The person usually prefers a muted color sedan for a car, and blues, grays, or browns for clothing. Not a single plaid will be found in their wardrobe. The gentleman who prefers high gloss finishes, thumbholes, and rollover combs on his rifles will often be seen wearing a Tartan print sweater, driving a sports car that is painted international orange. There is nothing wrong with either—it's just a matter of taste.

Most of all, the best reason for owning a custom rifle is that one wants to. No other reason is necessary.

Chapter 2

The Custom Stock

The most important feature of any custom firearm is its stock. That is one statement I believe will not be seriously challenged. So important is this one component that there are thousands of so-called custom rifles out there that have had nothing done to them other than the installation of a new stock. Technically, these rifles are not custom rifles, instead they are custom-stocked rifles. Let's not argue over semantics, though.

Thousands of dollars in labor devoted to magnificent and precise metal work is often overlooked. The stock, though, is always noticed, one way or the other. It is the stock that reaches out and grabs you, either positively or negatively. There are many facets of a custom stock that make it so distinctive. First is the material from which it is constructed. Second is the shape and styling. Third is the finish and checkering, and finally, the accessories or other decorations.

For many years, there was only one stock material—wood. There are many different types of wood that are suitable for making a stock, but only one is essentially ideal. That is one of the many sub-species of thin-shelled walnut (*Juglans regia*). Almost, but not quite, as good is American black walnut (*Juglans nigra*). Maple and mesquite have been used successfully, and many factory stocks on inexpensive firearms are made from other hardwoods that have been stained to look like walnut. Myrtle has been used as a raw material for stocks, and so have some exotic species such as koa, yama, and rosewood. The best of the stock woods, however, is still *Juglans regia*.

Although called by many names, French, Circassian, California English, and Turkish to name a few, it all comes from the same tree—only the location where it is grown and the growing conditions are different. France, Germany, Russia, Iran, Turkey, New Zealand, Morocco, and heaven only knows where else, have all provided excellent walnut for stocks. Each country has also, alas, provided some pretty sorry stuff. For an American, the source of some of the best stock blanks is the state of California. Usually called California English, it is readily available from a multitude of dealers. The best of it is so good that it will make a strong man cry.

One reason that California produces so much good wood is the cutters there generally know what they are doing when they cut logs into future gun stocks. This is often a failing in other locations. Some years ago, I saw a batch of blanks from Morocco. The wood was really beautiful, with superb figure and color, and it was also hard and dense; it had all the natural qualities required for superior stock blanks. Unfortunately, it was poorly cut, and for all practical purposes, was turned into very expensive firewood. It was really sad to see. I have seen the same problem with walnut cut in several different countries.

Another problem is that walnut is expensive.

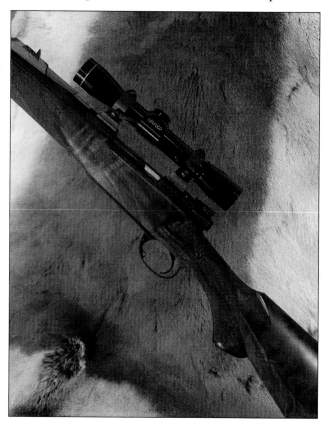

A small-ring Mexican Mauser action and a stick of beautiful French walnut were the starting components for this lovely rifle. Crafted by Bruce Russell, it also features a quarter-rib and scope mount bases fashioned by the maker from Damascus steel—a very unusual touch. This little .257 Roberts is capable of 1/2 MOA groups. Photo by Steven Dodd Hughes.

Because of this, many cutters minimize the size of the blanks, obviously to get more blanks out of a given log. By doing that, though, the stockmaker has little choice in laying out the stock. If the blank is not properly cut at the mill, there is usually no way to correct the mistake. In that case the blank becomes another expensive piece of firewood. Most of the California mills, however, seem to know what they are doing when cutting the blanks. Most don't leave any more excess wood to work with than the others, but they generally cut the blank correctly. It is important to remember that a beautiful and expensive blank is not necessarily a good one. The grain structure must be correct and if it isn't, a good stock cannot be made from the blank.

As an example, several years ago I started shivering and breaking out in night sweats, though the temperature was very mild. When my dog started howling at the moon due to my odd behavior, I knew there was a bout of customitis coming on. Except for a suitable stick of walnut, all the components for a custom rifle project to cure this malady were on hand. I saved a quarter here and there from my beer money allowance and eventually saved $100. That was the price for an AAA fancy European walnut blank—the price will give you an idea of how long ago this incident took place. I ordered the needed blank.

The stick I received was a beauty, with excellent figure and color. Sadly, it was very skimpily cut, with no maneuvering room to lay out the stock. As beautiful as it was, the blank was returned to the supplier. It was a spectacular piece of wood, hard and dense, but, whoever cut the blank had done so exactly upside down. The grain through what would become the grip of the stock, flowed precisely opposite to what it should have. Had that stick been made into a stock, it would have broken at the grip in no time. The supplier replaced the blank with another, not quite as beautiful, but infinitely better.

Claro walnut, also from California, is consistently beautiful wood. Unfortunately, it is normally also very porous and usually brittle, but I have seen some really gorgeous stocks crafted from Claro. Another type of walnut is a hybrid called Bastogne. It is hard and dense and makes excellent stocks for rifles chambered for heavy recoiling calibers. Bastogne is often rather plain in figure and not all that flashy, but really good stocks can be fashioned from it.

Curly maple has been used for stock wood since colonial times. It was apparently the favorite stock wood of our early rifle builders. The late Hal Hartley, a custom stock maker from North Carolina, specialized in making custom stocks from this wood. He made many of them and they were very good indeed. He most often used a blow torch to bring out the figure of the wood, called a Suigi finish. Curly maple

stocks are not often seen these days, though.

Roy Weatherby stocked most of his heavy caliber rifles in mesquite. In Arizona, where I live, the tree is common. It never grows very large, though, and where Weatherby found a source of trees large enough for stock blanks is a mystery to me. It was and is an interesting wood and the few stocks that I have seen fashioned from it were very good. The last time that I visited Frank Wells in his Tucson shop, he had a couple mesquite blanks on hand. I don't know where he got them because I didn't ask.

Arguably, the best material for a gunstock, particularly one that will be used and used hard, is not wood at all. Instead it is a combination of synthetic materials, which normally contains mostly fiberglass. Other materials, such as kevlar, are also used. These materials are inert and will not absorb moisture and will not swell, warp, crack, or shrink. They are impervious to the elements that affect wooden stocks so drastically. They aren't pretty, but they sure are practical for a working rifle. Generally, they have a painted finish and as such can be ordered in about any color one wants. Recently, however, a new method of finishing synthetic stocks has been devised that imparts a wood grain finish to the synthetic surface. A synthetic stock so finished is very difficult, even for an experienced observer, to distinguish from a fine walnut stock. It is only when it is handled that the difference is apparent.

The major objection that I have to a synthetic stock is that it has all the warmth and feel of a cadaver. Cheeking a synthetic stock, particularly on a cold day, is not one of life's greatest pleasures.

Somewhere between these stock extremes are stocks made from laminated wood blanks. They are made from many thin pieces of wood glued together under heavy pressure, similar to common plywood. The resultant blank has many advantages of both wood and synthetic stocks. A laminated stock resists the effects of moisture almost as well as a synthetic stock, but retains the warmth and feel of a fine wood stock. The only real failing is its appearance. When they first came out, most makers of the laminated blanks used alternating layers of walnut and maple. The resulting stock had the appearance of a zebra. Much more common today are blanks made from layers of walnut or other hard woods and, for my taste at least, they are much more attractive. Several custom makers are using laminated stocks on their semi-custom models and major manufacturers are also using them on selected production models.

The second important facet of a custom stock is its shape and styling. In broad terms, there are basically three categories, the so-called California style, the classic style, and what we will arbitrarily call the other style. Traditionally, Roy Weatherby has been

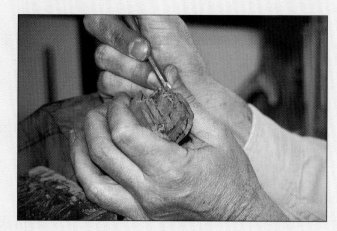

The stockmaking starts with the blank drilled for the through-bolt hole and milled for the tang inlets. The rough form of the wrist has been profiled with a bandsaw.

The head of the stock is progressively chiseled away to accept the action. Transfer blue is used to spot in the inletting showing the wood-to-metal fit.

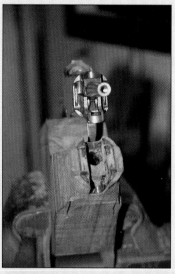

The action inletting is complete when there is 100 percent contact between the metal and wood.

Hughes uses a round gouge and a mallet to rough-in the barrel channel inlet. The channel is finished with smaller chisels and scrapers. An ebony forend tip has been installed.

At this stage, both the forend and buttstock blanks are completely inletted and installed to the barreled action. The gripcap and buttplate are also inletted and installed to help determine the stock shaping. After the blank has been bandsawn to profile, rough shaping lines are drawn on the quadrants of the butt.

Because of the fancy wood grain, the quadrants are first sawn, then a chisel and mallet are used to remove the bulk of the wood.

A pattern makers rasp is used to smooth and shape the contours. Here the grip contours are rasped to form.

The rifle is held firmly in a bench vise during the entire stockmaking process. Hughes is shaping the cheekpiece cove with a rasp.

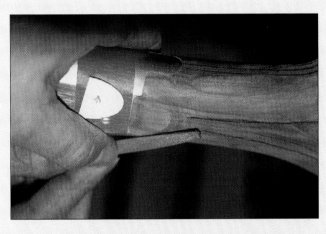

Subtle details such as the action panels shown here are created from the wood with a small course file.
A template is used to match the panels and finish shaping lines are drawn on the stock to help determine the flow of the stock.

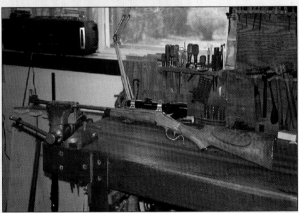

After rough shaping the stock, Hughes assembles the rifle to view the completed form.

This photo has the rifle completely disassembled to show all the pieces and parts of the project.

Sanding blends the stock lines and removes all of the tool marks prior to stock finishing.

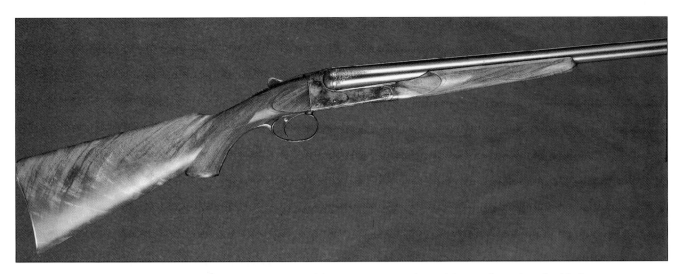

Starting a second hunting life as a used Winchester Model 21, it was transformed into a showpiece double by custom maker Bruce Russell and engraver Erich Gold. Russell completely reshaped and recontoured the action; he even fashioned several new parts for the gun. He then stocked it in a stick of genuine Circassian walnut. Gold embellished the rejuvenated Winchester with quail scenes and scrollwork. Photo by Steven Dodd Hughes.

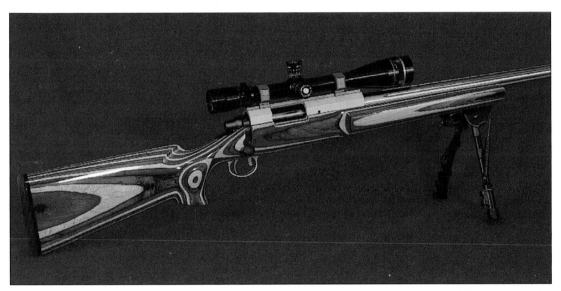

This example is unusual for a custom rifle, but custom it is in every respect. The red, white, and blue laminated stock is mated with a Remington 700 action hidden inside a 7075 T-6 aluminum sleeve. The sleeve is pillar bedded to the stock. The rifle is chambered for the 6mm Mashburn Improved cartridge and will push a 95 grain Ballistic Tip at 3,450 fps. All work by Bruce Russell and the photo is by Steven Dodd Hughes.

credited with popularizing the California influence in rifle stock design. Characterized by Monte Carlo combs, high gloss finishes, skip-a-line checkering patterns, angled forend tips, rollover cheekpieces, sharply curved pistol grips, and diamond shaped inlays, they were the cat's meow for awhile. They seemed to be most popular during the era when American automobiles featured fishtail fins and chrome plated everything. I don't know if the stock styling influenced the auto makers, or vice versa. It suffices to say that for several years, the style was very popular. The trend even moved to Europe and some European manufacturers produced rifles with stocks clearly

modeled after the California influence. Several custom makers, most notably Monty Kennedy, turned out fine custom stocks influenced by the California style.

The other category that I mentioned is even more bizarre, for my taste, than the California school. One of the most notable features of many of the other category of rifle stocks, is a thumbhole design. I will admit that the thumbhole stock is pretty comfortable, but personally, they aren't my cup of tea. The stock styling that has been around since colonial days is the classic style. There are as many different versions of this style as there are custom makers, but the differences are minor and the basics remain essentially the same, regardless of the maker. Perhaps the greatest proponent of the classic stock was Jack O'Connor. Any other stock styling gave him the "vapors." O'Connor wrote in his book *The Hunting Rifle*:

> Morgan Holmes, New Jersey stock maker, once wrote that the lines of a handsome rifle stock should either be straight or they should be segments of a circle. I think he has something there. I think also that the rifle stock should be judged not only by its utility but by the whole effect it gives. Any feature which detracts from the whole effect by attracting attention to itself is out of place. Any feature of the rifle stock that is put on for show and is plainly non-utilitarian also detracts from the overall beauty of a stock. That is why I do not care for carving, white spacers, gold plating, fancy inlays, and bizarre and exotic shapes. But anyone is entitled to spend his dough as the spirit moves him.

O'Connor, the master of words that he was, also wrote something else in the same book that I have always remembered. He wrote:

> Sometimes very slight changes in curves and angles make the difference between a beautiful and graceful stock and a homely and ordinary one. I am thinking now of two sisters I once knew. Both were blond, witty, and charming. But one (though she was a fine cook and had a heart of gold) was a rather ordinary-looking lass who got by on her good disposition and winning ways. The other was a tearing beauty, a creature so lovely that one look at her sent young men's blood pressure skyward and set them to uttering wild, hoarse cries and tearing telephone directories apart with their bare hands. Yet actually those two girls looked much alike. It was easy to see they were sisters. What made the difference was an angle here, a line there, small dimensional differences in eyes, noses, mouths.

So it is with many things, including custom gun stocks.

A properly executed classic-styled stock is utilitarian, efficient, unobtrusive, and quietly elegant. It min-

A most unusual Ruger No. 1 custom rifle: Metalsmith John Mandole converted the Ruger to a Rigby-style single-shot by eliminating the underlever and replacing it with a sidelever of his own creation. Extensively modified, the finished metalwork was given to Steven Dodd Hughes for a period style stock, a Hughes specialty. The engraved trim was executed by Mark Drain. Photo by Steven Dodd Hughes.

imizes the felt effects of recoil and never goes out of style. It requires no embellishment, save a well executed checkering job, to be beautiful. For my money, classic styling is the only way to go.

Checkering was originally strictly a utilitarian feature of a stock. It was added to a stock to improve the shooters' ability to grip the firearm firmly. Over the years, checkering has evolved into a decorative art form as well as a functional feature of a stock. A stock without checkering looks unfinished. Although there are an infinite number of variations, checkering patterns are basically one of two types—either a point or a fleur-de-lis pattern. I like both patterns and have examples of each type in my rack.

Point patterns have been around since there has been checkering on stocks. Just who originated the fleur-de-lis variation though, I'm not sure. It may have been Alvin Linden, or, if not, he was one of the first to use such a pattern on a stock. The fellow who made the pattern most famous, though, is Al Biesen. Biesen has used it so often that it has almost become a trademark with him. He undercuts the pattern, that

Called the Ladies Rifle by its creator, stockmaker Gary Goudy actually built the rifle for himself. Steve Heilmann shortened a Springfield action to match the intended 6mm PPC chambering as well as the other metalwork. Goudy fashioned the full-length stock to suit himself and then turned the project over to Sam Welch for the engraving. Photo by Mark Ross, courtesy of GUNS magazine.

is, he recesses the checkering below the surface of the wood. He is the only custom maker I know who does that. I think it looks spiffy.

Good checkering, running 22 to 26 lines per inch (LPI), is all the decoration a fine classic-styled stock needs. Checkering that is coarser than 22 LPI, while perhaps slightly more functional than the finer variety, is too coarse for my taste. Checkering finer than about 26 LPI loses its functional utility. Good checkering is characterized by a pattern where each diamond is identical in size and shape, and all the diamonds are sharpened to precise points. There are no flat diamonds in a good checkering job. Needless to say, runovers are not permitted and they stand out like a giraffe with a goiter if present! Borders around a pattern are generally frowned upon as a cover-up for runovers, and they can be. I do think that some point patterns look best with a simple border, though.

The only problem with checkering, other than poorly executed patterns, is that some makers use their outstanding checkering abilities to over-embel-lish an otherwise superb stock. Too many ribbons, arcs, and corners, while technically difficult to execute perfectly, tend to look overdone and out of place to my eyes. It reminds me of a farmer dressed in bib overalls who wears custom-made alligator boots! Individually, there is nothing wrong with bib overalls or alligator boots, but they just don't go together.

Neither do quietly elegant classic stocks and high gloss polyurethane finishes. No, classic stocks and hand-rubbed oil finishes go together like ham and eggs. In case you think I've been behind the moon for half my life, I do know that genuine oil finishes, linseed oil that is, are practically never used anymore. Technology has produced compounds that look just as good a genuine oil finish, but overcome the disadvantages of this finish. Pure oil finishes are beautiful and easy to repair, no doubt about that. Unfortunately, they do not effectively seal the stock from the elements. Also, an oil finish takes forever to dry, is soft, and much more prone to damage. Modern technology has developed various plastic "oils" that

The beginnings of a fine custom rifle are shown in this photo. A superb two-piece stick of walnut, a Hagn single-shot action and a Zeiss scope will eventually be crafted into something to behold. Photo by Mustafa Bilal.

provide the beautiful satin sheen of a hand-rubbed linseed oil finish and effectively fill the pores of the wood and drying to a hard, resistant surface. A perfect stock finish though, is the Holy grail of the custom gun business. I don't know any custom makers who are happy with the finish they use. Each is still looking for the perfect finish.

Wearing red and white argyle socks with a tuxedo would, to most observers, be considered out of place and inappropriate. To my way of thinking, so are white line spacers, exotic wood inlays (or even worse, ivory, pearl, or abalone shell), and zebra wood forend tips on a classic stock. Everything about the rifle must mesh and if something doesn't, it is inappropriate. A feature of the stock, if missing, should be noticed; not the other way around.

People have the right to spend their money on what they want. If a customer demands a stock whittled from grafted butternut, with an inlaid mother-of-pearl cheekpiece, why not? Somewhere out there, there is a maker who will give the customer what he or she wants. Gold inlaid maidens dressed in platinum bath towels are also available for the right price. If that is what an individual wants, that is what he or she should get. The fact that such a piece gives me hives just thinking about it is of no consequence. After all, it isn't my money. That is the beauty of the custom gun business. No matter how bizarre their tastes, all can get what they want.

Al Biesen told me a story once about the first stock job he did for Jack O'Connor. The year was, as I now recall, about 1947. The rifle O'Connor sent Biesen for stocking was a 1903 Springfield 30-06. Biesen worked his butt off getting everything just perfect on the job—as he always does. Because he had never worked for O'Connor before, he finished the stock with a high gloss finish and fitted white line spacers between the forend tip and the stock, as well as between the gripcap and the grip. O'Connor damned near birthed a litter of horned toads when he saw the finished job. He carped at Biesen for years afterward about it, even though that mistake was never repeated. In all fairness to Biesen, I saw the letter of instruction O'Connor sent along. There was no mention in it about stock finish or white line spacers.

For me, though, an elegant classic-styled stock from David Miller, Frank Wells, Al Biesen, Jerry Fisher, Gary Goudy, Duane Wiebe, Joe Balickie, or any number of other fine makers will do just fine. With any of these makers, it is guaranteed that I will get exactly what I want with not a single white line spacer—or red and white argyle sock—to be found anywhere.

Chapter 3

Custom Metalsmithing

I would guess that the most underrated component in building a custom gun is the metalsmithing. The stockwork immediately attracts attention. Fancy checkering patterns, meticulously executed, are sure to elicit oohs and aahs. A stock crafted from a beautifully figured and colored stick of walnut will snap heads from across the room. Yet, an integral quarter rib, front sight ramp, and sling swivel stud, machined from a single oversized barrel blank, hardly motivate a smile. The fact that a very talented 'smith spent many, many hours improving the workings of an already excellent action, often goes unnoticed. I suppose the aficionado simply expects the action to be glass smooth and function flawlessly. Believe me, it didn't get that way by accident!

The reason, I think, that superb metalwork goes largely unnoticed, is that much of the results of the work cannot be seen. Even if the work is visible, it is difficult to detect that a quarter rib has been machined from an oversized barrel blank. A quarter rib machined from a piece of bar stock and soldered to the barrel, if properly done, looks precisely the same. The same can be said for front sight ramps, sling swivel studs, extra recoil lugs on the barrel, and other touches.

Much of the action work is performed internally and greatly improves function, but not aesthetics.

Sometimes, but not often, an action is modified in appearance. Typically, a metalsmith will start with either a Model 98 Mauser or pre-64 Model 70 Winchester action. In most cases, the trigger and bottom metal—magazine box, floorplate, and trigger-guard—are removed and discarded. In the case of the Mauser, the safety will be replaced with a Model 70 type side-swing model. The bolt handle will be cut off and replaced with a new one.

In some shops, the action is tested for hardness and sent to specialists for a new heat treatment. Often, Mauser actions are too soft to suit many makers. By contrast, the pre-64 Model 70 is sometimes too hard. In both cases, the solution is a new tempering process, performed by experts specializing in this process. I once wrote a magazine article in which I mentioned that custom makers sometimes retemper actions. One reader, a former employee of a US gun manufacturer, took me to task. His thesis was that only the manufacturer of an action should attempt to retemper an action. Of course, that is good advice, when practical and possible. In my response to his letter, I told him that I seriously doubted that Mauser would accept a sixty year old WWII military action

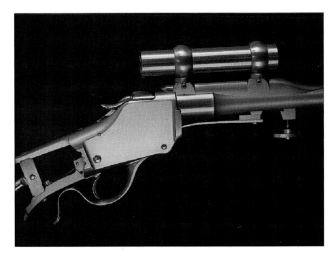

A completely reworked Winchester High Wall action from the shop of Steve Heilmann. In addition to the work on the action, Heilmann also fashioned the quarter-rib and scope mount base system.
Photo by Steven Dodd Hughes.

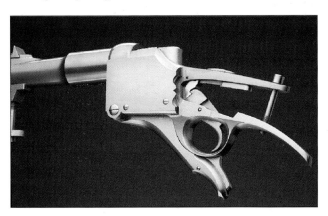

Outstanding metalwork just doesn't get any better than the work on this Farquharson by Steve Heilmann. Equally adept at stockmaking, Heilmann is truly a do-it-all gunmaker. Photo courtesy of Steve Heilmann.

back at its plant for that purpose. I expressed further doubt that United States Repeating Arms Corporation (USRAC), the successor to Winchester firearms manufacturing, would take in a pre-64 Model 70 action for retempering.

I also explained to the gentleman that the process I described did not rely on a can of oil and a blow torch!

The companies that perform these services are equipped with highly controllable equipment that cost megabucks and they employ professional metallurgists. Most of them are as well if not better equipped for the task than the original manufacturer. In the end, my critic and I agreed on most items of contention and agreed to disagree on a couple of others.

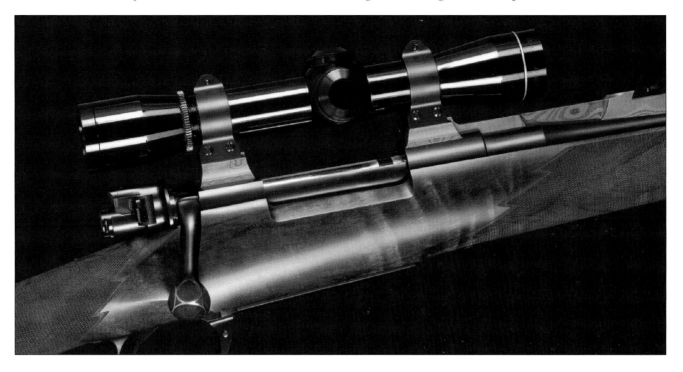

Both the metal and stockwork on this lovely little .257 Roberts were executed by Bruce Russell. Of particular note are the quarter-rib and scope mount bases. They are crafted from Damascus steel—a very unusual combination. Photo by Steven Dodd Hughes.

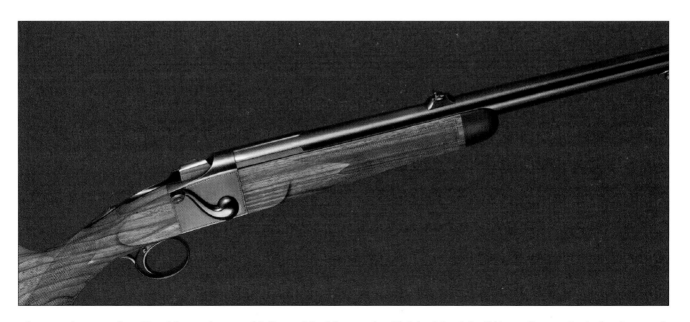

A tremendous metalworking job was done on this Ruger No. 1 by metalsmith John Mandole. Of immediate notice is the absence of the normal Ruger underlever, that Mandole replaced with a sidelever. Mandole also crafted a new trigger and triggerguard for the rifle along with numerous other, less noticeable, modifications. The stock and the photo are by Steven Dodd Hughes.

Anyway, once the maker is satisfied with the temper of the action, he or she will usually replace the trigger with a preferred commercially manufactured one. The maker will then turn to Dakota Arms, Jim Wisner, or Ted Blackburn for new bottom metal. A few 'smiths make their own bottom metal, but most find the task too time consuming to be profitable and buy a replacement from a specialist. The same is true of bolt handles. The military Mauser bolt handle is always either replaced or reshaped. As issued, the Mauser crank cannot be used with a scope and few rifles are not so equipped these days. The solution is to lop off the original bolt handle and weld on a new replacement. Here again, most 'smiths buy their replacement bolt handles from Wisner, Brownells, or other suppliers, but a few make their own variety.

The trigger receives much attention and insures a smooth, clean break with no creep. Knowing where and how much to hone will take care of that task. The action is also a recipient of the honing process. The bolt and the action recesses are honed until the bolt will practically fall open by itself. Often, makers will machine a new follower tailored for the specific caliber of the rifle. They will always devote a great deal of attention to feeding. They will feed dummy cartridges through the magazine into the action time and time again, and hone here and polish there, until smooth, trouble-free feeding is achieved.

Some of our really talented metalsmiths will either shorten or lengthen an action to suit a particular need. Magnum-length Mauser actions are scarce and expensive when one can be found for sale. The petite original Mauser *kurz* (short) actions are even rarer. If a maker needs an action of rare length for a project, the least expensive solution, although still not cheap, is to either make one or have one made.

Skilled metalsmiths start with a couple inexpensive military Mauser 98 actions. Very simplistically described, they basically cut a piece from one action and weld it onto the second, thereby lengthening one and shortening the other. One maker told me that he uses three standard actions to end up with one short

The tang extension was fashioned by welding on an additional metal strap and then shaping the new piece to match the existing tang. Frank Wells did the work in his Tucson shop.

The beginnings of a custom quarter-rib added to a heavy caliber magazine rifle. When finished, this quarter-rib will serve as a base to fit an English-type folding leaf express sight. The work is being done by Frank Wells.

Gunmaker Frank Wells at his mill, converting an oversized round barrel into an octagon shape. Enough steel will be left oversized on the barrel to fashion an integral quarter-rib, front sling swivel base, and front sight ramp.

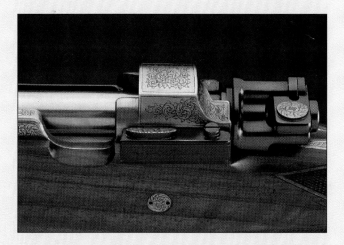

Some exceptional metalwork adorns this Argentine 1909 Mauser action: Steve Heilmann did the metalsmithing which was later adorned by the fabulous engraving of Ron Smith. Photo by Mustafa Bilal.

and one long finished action—the third action serves essentially as a spare parts bin for the process. Steve Heilmann, on the other hand, uses but two actions and ends up with two. I have seen numerous actions that have been modified using this technique and, if properly done, it is undetectable short of X-ray investigation.

A few original Mauser sporting rifles were built with raised and flattened metal platforms on the rear or front action bridges and sometimes both. I presume this was done to facilitate scope mounting on the actions. Original square bridge Mausers, as they are called, are rare and very desirable to collectors. Making a single or double square bridge action is no problem for a skilled metalsmith. He merely welds on added metal to the action bridges and shapes the added material to the desired contours.

The barrel also receives substantial metalwork. In addition to the already mentioned integral quarter rib, front sight ramp, and sling swivel stud, the shape of the barrel itself is often modified. Sometimes, the

barrel will be machined to an octagonal shape rather than round. Every now and then, a maker will combine both round and octagonal shapes in the same barrel. If the quarter rib, front sight ramp, and sling swivel stud are not integral, and they usually aren't, then they are machined separately from bar stock and soldered to the barrel. A trend that I have noted lately from a few makers is to fashion the rib and ramp from a piece of Damascus steel rather than bar stock. One job from Bruce Russell I saw had the quarter rib, front sight ramp, and also scope mount bases made of Damascus steel. I think it looks spiffy, though there is no functional advantage that I know of for doing so.

Many of our best metalsmiths are also quite young in years. Heck, I still have socks older than Mark Cromwell and Rick Stickley. The quality of the work they turn out though, is mind numbing. One of the best, Steve Heilmann, is still a young man. It is scary to think how good they might be when they get a little gray behind the ears. A couple guys that have gotten a bit gray around the sides are Herman Waldron

This Model 21 Winchester action is about to undergo a transformation in the shop of Steven Dodd Hughes. He starts the work by polishing the action with various grits of polishing cloth. Photo by Steven Dodd Hughes.

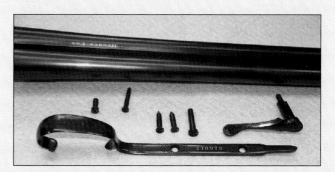

Rust blued barrels, charcoal blued guard and lever, along with nitre blued screws, are the appropriate finishes for fine custom shotguns. These various finishes were performed by Doug Turnbull. Photo by Steven Dodd Hughes.

When a factory or original trigger just won't work for a given project, some 'smiths merely fashion a new one at the bench that will. Steve Hughes made this one from scrap stock that he had available in the shop. Photo by Steven Dodd Hughes.

Hand filing is the only way to shape the subtleties of a shotgun action. This Fox gun is in the initial stages of extensive cosmetic modification by Steven Dodd Hughes. Photo by Steven Dodd Hughes.

and Bob Snapp. Both turn out exquisite metalwork. Another is Ted Blackburn. Although Blackburn is better known for his custom bottom metal, when it comes to metalwork, he can do it all.

The team of David Miller and Curt Crum—the David Miller Company—compliment each other nicely. Makers of one of the finest custom rifles in the universe, Miller does mostly metalwork these days while Crum does mostly stockwork. Even so, Miller can turn out an excellent stock if necessary and Crum can do all the metalworking chores. They can also produce accessories, exhibition quality oak-and-leather trunk cases, and about anything else known to man. They don't make their own actions although they could. The action that they use in their guns today, the current Winchester (USRAC) Super Grade Model 70, was in large measure developed in the Miller shop. How it came about is an interesting story.

In the early 1980s, Miller and Safari Club International (SCI) came up with the idea of produc-

This snazzy trap gripcap is about as nicely done as any you'll ever see. It is a combination of the talents of metalsmith Steve Heilmann and engraver Ron Smith. Photo by Mustafa Bilal.

ing five custom rifles, one per year, each dedicated to one of the big five game animals of Africa. The Elephant Rifle, built by Miller and Crum, was the first. That was followed by the Champlin Rhino Rifle, Heym's Buffalo Rifle, Jaeger's Lion Rifle, and finally the Leopard Rifle, again from the Miller shop. As the finale to the series, Miller wanted to do something extraordinary. In coordination with USRAC, the Miller shop developed a new Model 70 action that combined the best of the features of the pre-64 action with those of the post-64 action. USRAC then produced a tool-room prototype and sent it to Tucson. I was present in the shop when the package was opened.

It was nowhere near a finished action as Miller received it. The parts were roughly machined, but no fitting had been done nor, as memory serves me now, had the action been heat-treated. The Miller shop did all the fitting, honing, and polishing on the action then returned it to USRAC for heat treatment. This unique action was then used to craft the Leopard Rifle which sold at auction for the whopping sum of $201,000. That was a record at the time for a modern bolt action rifle, and, I believe, probably still is. There is some debate as to whether the Leopard Rifle or the first rifle in a second, later SCI series of guns, holds the record.

The Grizzly Rifle, magnificently crafted by John Bolliger and Rick Stickley, sold for more money at auction—$225,000—than did the Leopard Rifle. The Grizzly Rifle price, however, included an original 400 ounce .999 silver sculpture by Dennis Jones and a glorious walnut credenza expertly constructed by Tom Julian. For that reason, it is difficult to say which piece truly holds the record. It is not at all difficult to state, though, that both pieces are among the finest ever built.

With the computer-controlled machinery available today, it is perhaps easier to do quality metalwork

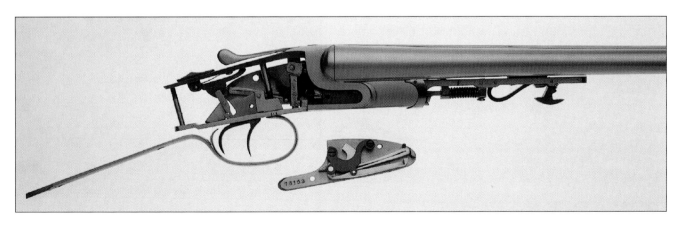

Starting with an old L.C. Smith shotgun, metalsmith Pete Mazur converted the old gun into a modern piece with his outstanding work. This photo was taken when the Smith was well along toward completion, but not yet totally finished. Photo by Mustafa Bilal.

Metalsmith Gary Stiles built this Mauser action sporter with a takedown feature. Not only does this feature enable carrying the rifle in a much smaller package, but Stiles also fitted the rifle with interchangeable barrels. He does outstanding work in his Pennsylvania shop. Photo by Mark Ross, courtesy of GUNS magazine.

than ever before. But, and it is a huge but, how many custom shops can afford such a piece of technology? Few, if any, I suspect. In addition, such equipment is really only practical if a series of like pieces are being produced. A factory that produces one piece after the other, all precisely alike, can and must use such expensive machinery. An individual maker who almost never produces the identical product twice gains no advantage in doing so.

Almost every shop has a lathe and a mill, but much of the work is done with files, scrapers, and stones. That technology has been around since well before the industrial revolution. Still, they do the job and do it well, provided the user has the necessary skills. I am reminded that the test for a German apprentice gunsmith to graduate to the journeyman level used to be to convert a block of steel to an action, using nothing but files. For all I know, that is still a requirement.

One component of custom metalwork is becoming so specialized that it has almost developed into a separate discipline. This component is metal finishing. Not long ago, we basically had bluing. Most 'smiths used the hot blue process on highly polished metal. The resultant was a high gloss blue job, acceptable to most clients. In the last several years, though, high

gloss has lost out in many circles to a soft matte blue. The hot blue process is still widely used, but the old fashioned rust blue process has been resurrected.

These days we have hot blue, rust blue, niter blue, charcoal blue, differential blue, and probably a couple others I haven't yet heard of. Another ancient form of metal finishing that has been rescued from oblivion is color case hardening. Years ago, the process was necessary because the available steels of the period were not nearly as technically advanced as those in use today. The process hardened the steel to an acceptable level and added beautiful coloring to the material. No longer necessary to strengthen the steel, it has been rescued from the scrap heap for the beautiful coloring it provides.

There is no question that we are seeing much better metalwork in custom guns today than at any point in our past. Advances in technology can account for some of the improvements, but by no means all. I suspect that the primary reason is simply that makers have developed a customer base that is willing to pay for their added efforts. Precise metalwork is labor intensive and time consuming. By and large, the work is less noticeable to the average potential buyer and until relatively recently, these customers were unwilling to pay for it. Thanks to projects such as those of Safari Club International, the American

Custom Gunmakers Guild, and other similar organizations, this has changed.

Projects such as the SCI sponsored events basically gave the participating makers a free hand, mostly unrestricted by cost considerations. As such, they were free to show what they were capable of, not necessarily what they could sell. This situation provided a continuing education for both makers and potential customers alike. Makers would be able to see what their competitors were turning out and could react to it as a challenge. The potential clients for a custom job, by seeing more and more quality work, raised their standards for what they would accept. Equally important is that they also raised the amount that they were willing to pay for the work. This combination has raised the quality of the custom gun of today all across the board.

While I believe that the quality of work has improved in every aspect, I maintain that our metalsmiths have shown the most dramatic increases in technical virtuosity. Even though their work is somewhat less appreciated by the general aficionado, they continue to strive towards perfection.

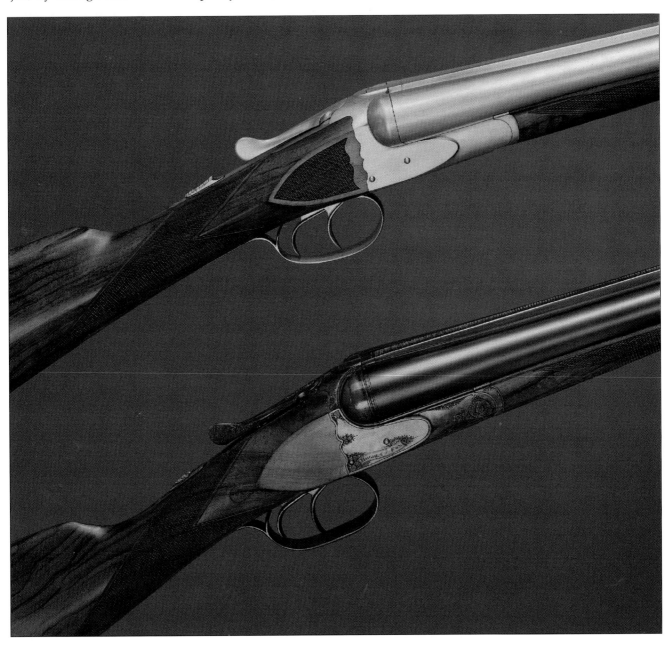

Two examples of the work of Steven Dodd Hughes. The top gun is an extensively modified Fox shotgun that is not yet quite finished. The bluing and engraving of the gun are yet to be done. The bottom example is finished, complete with engraving by Eric Gold. Hughes did both the metal and stockwork on these two guns. Photo by Steven Dodd Hughes.

Chapter 4

Actions

This scribe is a great fan of the Pre-64 Winchester Model 70 action for my custom rifles. All sorts of functional and aesthetic reasons for this preference could be given, such as looks, controlled round feeding, side swing safety, smooth functioning (sometimes with a little help), etc. To be completely honest, though, the real reason I favor this great action over Mauser, Remington, Enfield, or any number of other perfectly acceptable actions, can be blamed on one man, Jack O'Connor.

As a kid growing up, I had never heard of Ernest Hemingway or Robert Ruark. I read many great classic authors such as Shakespeare, Longfellow, and Dante, not because I particularly enjoyed their work, but because my English and Literature teachers required it of me. The great writers I read for enjoyment and to learn a thing or two from were Pete Brown of *Sports Afield*, Warren Page of *Field & Stream*, and I think the best of all, Jack O'Connor of *Outdoor Life*. If I didn't have enough money to pick up all three magazines at the local drugstore, I bought *Outdoor Life* first, followed by whatever my meager allowance would

A pretty good assortment of actions and barreled actions used in building a fine custom rifle. These include former military hardware as well as commercially produced models.

allow. Always first, though, was *Outdoor Life*. The reason was that O'Connor wrote exclusively for that magazine.

O'Connor influenced me in many ways, some immediately, and others not until later. One of his early impressions on me was his choice of rifle styling

and his selection of the Model 70 Winchester action, pre-64 of course, to send off to Al Biesen for another fine custom rifle. How I longed in those days to have Biesen build me a rifle identical with one of O'Connor's. I still have that longing although I have not, to date, been able to satisfy the desire. Biesen is now more than seventy-five years young and is still going strong. Perhaps before he turns one hundred, I can realize my long running dream.

Nevertheless, the pre-64 Model 70 Winchester is a wonderful action. Engineered with many features of the Mauser, a Model 70 also contains refinements that have to be added to Peter Paul's great development to improve it. At least three significant changes are routinely made to a Mauser action when using it as the basis for a fine custom rifle. First, the safety is replaced. The Mauser original has a very positive safety that locks the firing pin. Unfortunately, it is also pretty cumbersome to use, particularly when the rifle has a scope. Custom 'smiths customarily replace it with a copy of the Model 70 safety. Second, the original Mauser two-stage trigger is either replaced or substantially modified to eliminate the first stage military pull. Finally, the bolt handle must either be replaced or reshaped to permit the low mounting of a scope.

Some Mauser actions, particularly the late production military ones, tend to be a bit soft. According to Ludwig Olson in his great book *Mauser Bolt Rifles*, Mauser actions were produced from carbon steel with a relatively soft inner core and hardened outer surface. Also, Olson reported that various parts of the action were heat treated differently, according to the stress and wear to which a given part would be subjected. Apparently in the turmoil of the late war years, heat treatment, among other things, was not always well done. With the high pressure cartridges often chambered today, it would be wise for makers to always check the hardness of the action used, particularly if it is a late WWII production Mauser military model.

The Mauser Model 98 type action is, without question, the most popular action in the world and has been for many, many years. Very few bolt actions have been manufactured since the introduction of the Model 98 that did not liberally borrow from Peter Paul's design. Some are direct copies, while others are modified in some manner. In general, though, most actions on the market are principally Mauser in function. Some of the finest custom rifles ever built have been put together using Mauser actions and that continues today.

One feature of the Mauser action that has received much hoopla is called controlled round feeding. It is a most desirable feature. Essentially what happens is

Two magnum-length Mauser action clones: At the top is the investment cast BBK-02 action. Below it is a machined left-hand action made in the US by Crandall Tool & Machine Co.

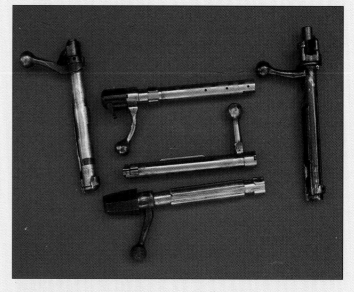

Several bolts encountered on custom rifle actions. At the left is a pre-64 Winchester Model 70 and on the right, a magnum Mauser bolt. In between, at the top, is the Schultz & Larsen rear locking bolt, in the middle a military Mauser Model 98 bolt and on the bottom, a Champlin bolt.

that the round that comes up from the magazine is fed under the extractor of the bolt. The extractor firmly holds the round and directs it, under the control of the bolt, into the chamber. The cartridge remains under positive control of the bolt from the time it leaves the magazine until it is firmly seated in the chamber. The modern series of actions strip the round from the magazine in the same manner, but leaves it loose in the action. It is pushed along by the bolt travel but is under no control at all. For obvious reasons, the controlled feed is vastly preferable. I know of but one disadvantage to controlled round feeding—that is in a situation where a hunter is in the middle of a contest with a dangerous animal. If the hunter uses all the ammo in the magazine and tries to simply drop a cartridge into the chamber and close the bolt quickly, there can be a problem. Particularly with original Mauser actions, it is difficult and sometimes practically impossible to close the bolt. The reason is that the action is designed to feed the cartridge from the magazine. To chamber a round without feeding it through the magazine, it is necessary to snap the large ejector over the cartridge head. That can be done, with difficulty, with some controlled round feed actions. With an original Mauser, though, it is damned near difficult, if not impossible, to do.

One measure of the 98 type action popularity is the number of different manufacturers that have produced essentially a direct copy of it. I won't bore the reader with an exhaustive listing, but such actions have been produced in France, Belgium, Spain, Yugoslavia, South America, Korea, and the USA, just to name a few. Probably the most famous versions, other than the original, were turned out by Fabrique Nationale in Belgium and Brevex in France.

About three years ago, there was a surprising resurrection of the .416 Rigby, along with several other .416 caliber ballistic clones. Remington came out with one, as did Weatherby. Ruger decided to stay with the old tried and true Rigby version, and so did Kimber and Heym. Dakota chambered rifles for both the original Rigby and the Remington. These were added to a couple .416 caliber wildcats that had been kicking around for quite some time. The .416 Taylor, based on a necked down .458 case and the .416 Hoffman, based on a blown out .375 case, each essentially duplicated the original Rigby ballistics, but at considerably higher pressures. The Remington version is almost identical to George Hoffman's baby, and why the Big Green didn't just offer it instead of developing its version is a mystery. Weatherby, typical of his philosophy, wasn't satisfied with the perfectly adequate 2,370 feet per second (fps) muzzle velocity produced by the other .416s. The Weatherby version was souped up to

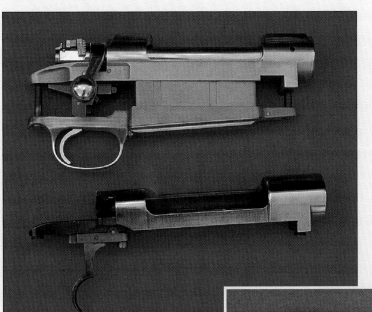

An original magnum Mauser action well on its way to being turned into a modern custom rifle. Much work remains to be done, but it will become a fine rifle when finished.

When the big bore craze hit shooters, there was a shortage of long magnum-length actions to accommodate the demand. The BBK-02 action at the top was one manufacturer's effort to meet the demand. Investment cast in Korea, the first few actions were pretty rough. Later versions were pretty good actions and many were used to build large bore magazine rifles. It was a copy of the Brno Mauser action with some added refinements. Below the BBK is another commercial Mauser action in wide use. It was produced by FN in Belgium.

43

An original magnum Mauser action as used by John Rigby for one of that prestigious firm's rifles. When it left the factory, this rifle was chambered for the .350 Rigby magnum cartridge. Later, it was returned to Rigby and converted to the more popular .375 H&H magnum.

a sizzling 2,700 fps.

Anyway, the purpose in this .416 dissertation is that while the Remington, Taylor, and Hoffman varieties could be chambered in a .375 H&H length action, the Rigby and Weatherby versions could not. They required a true magnum-length action and bolt head diameter. When Brevex stopped production of its magnum action, there were few available actions large enough to handle such a cartridge. The Weatherby Mark V would, but other than lucking on an original magnum Mauser, either the Oberndorf or Brevex varieties, precious few alternatives remained. The .416 mania cured that problem.

Three magnum-length Mauser clones. At the top is the Brno ZKK-602 action, middle a BBK-02 action, and on the bottom, a USA made custom left-hand Mauser copy by Crandall Tool & Machine Co.

Ruger developed its version of a magnum-sized action and wrapped a .416 Rigby chambered rifle around it. Dumoulin from Belgium had a massive action for a .416 Rigby-sized cartridge. Heym of Germany developed its own action, and typical of the Germans, did everyone one better. It even chambered its Heym Express for the .600 Nitro Express! Don Allen of Dakota produced his Dakota 76 action in the appropriate size, as did Kimber before it went belly up. Of this group, the Ruger was the least expensive, although I don't know if just an action can be obtained from Ruger. Price wise, Dakota was next. The Dumoulin and Heym actions are wonderful, but terribly expensive.

Not to worry—along came the BBK 02 action. Investment cast and imported from Korea, this action was on the market for around $500, and many .416 Rigbys were built on it. The earliest examples of the action were a bit on the rough side, but later examples I saw were pretty good. Even the rough examples were perfectly satisfactory, after a bit of polishing and honing. Unfortunately, I understand the BBK is no longer in production. Fortunately, the rest of them still are. Several 'smiths I know bought Brno ZKK-602 rifles when they could find one. This Czech-made rifle has a Mauser type magnum-length action. While it is rather roughly made as it comes from the factory, the basics are there. By making a few modifications to the action, replacing the trigger and bottom metal, and a few hours honing and polishing, the resulting action is excellent.

As I'm sure most readers know already, the original Mauser was manufactured in several different lengths. I'm not a Mauser collector and am not really up on all the different varieties, but I do know that there were short actions, standard-length actions, and magnum-length actions. Apparently, the rarest variety was the *kurz*, or short action. I know that in a lifetime of nosing around gun shops and gun shows, I have seen very few of them. Original magnum-length actions are also scarce and expensive.

The vast majority of actions commonly used today use front locking bolts. By that I mean that the locking lugs on the bolt are at the front, just behind the chamber when engaged. The number of lugs vary depending on the action. Some have two massive locking lugs and use the bolt handle as a third lug, and others have as many as nine much smaller lugs. Mauser is the best example of the former and the Weatherby Mark V, the latter.

Back in the 1950s, or at least it was about that time when I became aware of it, the Danish firm Schultz & Larsen marketed a rifle in the US. This rifle used a different concept. The locking lugs on the bolt of this Scandinavian import were toward the rear of the bolt shaft. There may have been other rear locking actions around, but as memory serves me now, the Dane product was the first such action I can remember coming across. Since then, several other rear locking actions have come on the market, although I don't believe any were all that successful. Most that I am aware of were European models, although a couple were produced in Japan. Remington had a rear locking model for awhile, the Model 788.

Rear locking bolt actions can be made velvety smooth in their function and with very short bolt throws. Both attributes are desirable. Unfortunately, for a reloader at least, they had one perceived disqualifying factor. I say perceived because I have never used a rear locking bolt action rifle enough to experience the problem. Apparently, since the bolt head is not physically supported, the pressure generated by the cartridge firing springs the bolt head slightly to the rear. The flexing is very, very slight, but ostensibly sufficient to permit the brass cartridge case to stretch slightly. I suspect this fault, real or perceived, had a great deal to do with the lack of success of this type action. Whether it is a bum rap or not, I can't say. I can say that rear locking actions haven't been very popular with the shooting public.

No article on rifle actions would be complete without mention of actions other than bolts. The purely American innovation, the lever action, has lost much of its popularity in recent years. Typified by the Model 94 Winchester, the lever gun is still very practical and useful in some hunting situations. So are semi-autos and pump action rifles still in production. Remington produces both types and Browning has its semi-auto. The single shot rifle, with a Ruger No. 1, the best example, is very popular, even today. I have three in my personal battery, and use them frequently. Except for the single shot though, precious little custom work is done on any non-bolt action rifles.

Which action is best as the basis for a custom rifle? I'll

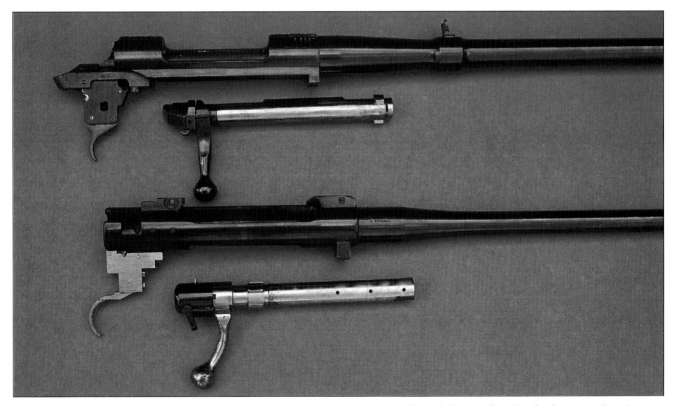

Shown here are two actions that are seldom seen these days. At the top is a BSA barreled action from England. At one time, it was used by Herter's as the basis for their rifle. Below it is the Schultz & Larsen barreled action. Notice that the Schultz & Larsen has a rear locking bolt. Both were imported into the US in fair numbers in the 1960s.

cop out and say whichever you prefer. Answering that question otherwise would surely fill my mail box quickly. As I said in the beginning of this chapter, I personally prefer the pre-64 Model 70 action as the basis for my rifles. Having said that, though, I currently have a couple custom jobs in the works and neither project is using that action. Both of my present ongoing projects are being built around 98 Mauser actions. I had two fine pre-war actions on hand and decided to use them rather than try to find, and more importantly come up with, the cash necessary to buy a couple of Model 70s. I can't wait to see and use the finished products. I know that they will work just fine.

Since USRAC came out with the current Super Grade Model 70 action, there is little justification, other than nostalgia and stubbornness, to track down a pre-64 variety. The current production model is excellent and in several ways, superior to the earlier Model 70 action. I wish I had a footlocker full of them.

Not many Springfield '03 actions are used anymore for custom rifles. Many excellent rifles in the past were built around the action, though, and numerous fine makers cut their teeth converting Springfield actions to inexpensive sporting rifles. Modern custom jobs on this action are, however, seldom seen today. Still, California stockmaker Gary Goudy recently built a wonderful little rifle using a Springfield action. Goudy sent the action to Steve Heilmann and had it shortened by half an inch or so. He barreled it and chambered the rifle for the 6mm PPC cartridge. He then sent the rifle to engraver Sam Welch for a magnificent engraving job. Goudy stocked the rifle to the muzzle 'a la Mannlicher with a super stick of walnut. Finally, Marvin Huey cased the rifle in one of his superb oak-and-leather-type trunk cases. When I asked Goudy why he chose to use the Springfield action, he replied, "just to be different."

I once owned a custom rifle made by Texas maker Cecil Weems. Weems used a Shilen action for the rifle and chambered it for a really odd duck, the .270/08. The Shilen action was wonderful and Weems metal and stock work was excellent. I never used the rifle much, though, primarily because of the caliber. I eventually traded the rifle for something, although I can't remember what.

The 1917 Enfield action was a popular choice for magnum cartridges for a long time. The action had enough beef to it to permit opening it up to accommodate .375 H&H length cartridges. On the down side, the

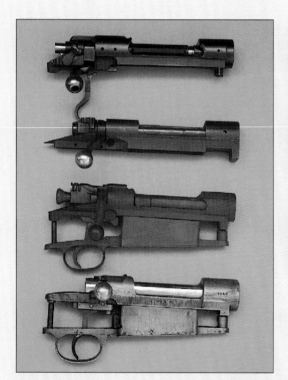

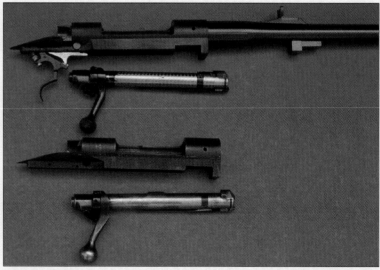

Two Winchester Model 70 actions: At the top is a recent production action and below it, the famous pre-64 Model. In my opinion, the currently produced model (with controlled round feeding) is every bit as good and in some ways superior to the pre-64 version.

These four actions are probably the most commonly used to craft custom rifles: From top to bottom, a 1917 Enfield, pre-64 Model 70 Winchester, 1903 Springfield, and the Model 98 Mauser.

action took a substantial amount of work to convert it to an aesthetically pleasing action. Even with all the work necessary, they were commonly seen. One company, A-Square, still uses this action on its large bore rifles.

Surprisingly, an action that I have rarely seen on a custom rifle is the Weatherby Mark V. Why, I can't say. There is no doubt that it is a strong and smooth action and in factory form has been a very successful rifle. Yet, I have only seen one or two custom jobs built around this action.

One of my biggest surprises concerning actions took place during a visit to the famed British rifle maker John Rigby. This was during the late 1970s when the firm was still at the old Pall Mall Street address and not doing very well financially. A potential client came in and inquired about having a stalking rifle built. The young gunmaker discussing the project with him was recommending a military Mannlicher action! I can't imagine a more inappropriate action for a fine British rifle than a surplus Mannlicher. I would have been no more surprised had I been visiting a Rolls Royce showroom and overheard a salesman recommending a Volkswagen engine for its Silver Shadow!

Of all the custom rifles being built today as well as most of them built in the past, Winchester and Mauser actions dominate the field. I have seen a few custom jobs using Remington Model 700 actions, but not many. These days, a few Dakota 76 actions are showing up on custom rifles, but cosmetically, the 76 is very similar to the Model 70.

I suspect the reasons for the predominance of Model 70 and Mauser actions are many. Availability is an issue, and Mausers are both common and inexpensive. Model 70s are also available, but at higher prices. Both actions can be turned into very attractive actions. The Model 70 requires a lot less work than does the Mauser. Many makers use the Model 70 as is, with little added work other than cleaning and polishing. The Mausers, on the other hand, all require a substantial amount of work to get them ready to use. Either way, most custom rifles sport one of these two action types. The major reasons are that they look good, are very strong, and they work well. I suspect we will continue to see these two action types dominate the custom rifle field.

This action is seldom encountered on the custom market except directly from its manufacturer. Champlin offers complete rifles based upon this action and it is a very good one.

A key component in the crafting of a custom rifle is a good action. Shown here are several good ones that are often used. Clockwise, from the left, are the BBK-02, 1917 Enfield, Winchester Model 70, USA made left-hand Mauser clone by Crandall, and a commercial Mauser. In the middle at the top is a 1903 Springfield action. Below it is a military Mauser Model 98.

47

Chapter 5

Barrels

There is a saying in golf which goes, "you drive for show and putt for dough." For the non-golfer, the adage means that a long, straight drive off the tee and down the middle of the fairway, while impressive to watch, doesn't get the ball in the hole. It is largely the putter and not the driver that accounts for low scoring. To play really well, of course, all facets of one's game must be solid. The same principle can be applied to rifles.

We can equate the driver to a rifle stock. It is the showy part of a custom rifle. It is the first thing that any observer notices and is the one aspect of a custom rifle that practically everyone uses to arrive at a judgment on the quality of the piece. Naturally, it is important. But, just as the score in golf depends largely on the putter, the accuracy of a rifle depends mostly on the barrel. A good drive certainly contributes to the score, just as a properly bedded stock promotes accuracy. The best drive in the world, however, won't get the golf ball into the hole. Likewise, the best stock in the world won't, by itself, result in one-hole groups!

As we shall see, there are many variables in a rifle barrel. A barrel in its most elementary form, is merely a billet of steel with a very straight hole drilled through it. The hole is, by one of a number of methods, then provided with rifling. Rifling is simply a series of grooves that spiral through the barrel at a prescribed rate of twist. This rate is

Barrels differ substantially in weight, length, and contour: Shown here at the top is a barrel blank that is, as yet, not threaded for an action. It could be contoured into a sporter weight barrel or left as is for a varmint rifle. Below it is a barrel that has been contoured, chambered, and threaded for an action. It will be used on a hunting rifle.

generally measured and related as 1:10, 1:12, etc. This means, in the case of 1:10, that the rifling makes one complete turn every 10 inches. For 1:12, the turn takes 12 inches, and so on. Once the hole is drilled and the rifling added, all that remains to finish the barrel is to contour the outside surface of the steel, cut threads on one end, and ream the chamber for a given caliber. It can then be screwed into an action, properly head-spaced, and taken to the range. Naturally, this description is a very simplified rendition of what actually takes place. Fundamentally, though, the characterization is accurate.

Barrels these days are fabricated from one of two general types of steel, either chrome-moly or stainless. I'm not a metallurgist and I seriously doubt if the reader is either. Therefore, I'll leave the steel composition at that. I will only say that there are several formulas for each type, with differing percentages of this and that element employed in making the steel. For practical purposes, however, they are all fundamentally the same. About the only thing that I have learned the hard way is that European-produced stainless steel, particularly German made, contains a higher percentage of chrome than does US stainless. As a result, European stainless barrels are considerably more difficult to work with. Unless users are well-equipped and really know what they are doing, they probably should leave them alone. Once threaded, chambered, and installed, they are excellent barrels. Performing these necessary tasks, though, can drive a Baptist preacher to drink.

In general, there are three methods of producing the rifling in the barrel. Each method has its proponents that swear by a given method, and its detractors that swear at the same method. There are also variations of each method. For our purposes, though, discussing the three broadly is sufficient. These three methods are cut rifling, button rifling, and hammer-forged rifling.

Cut rifling is the oldest method and remains very popular even today. Many makers feel that an expertly made cut rifled barrel is the best of all. Simplistically, such a barrel is produced by placing a hook-shaped cutter on the end of a long rod. A gearing device is attached to the rod that causes it to turn at a precise and prescribed rate. By making repeated passes through the bore with the cutter and removing a small amount of steel with each pass, the maker will eventually cut the grooves to the proper depth. Once the cutting is finished, the bore, with its newly formed rifling, is lapped to remove any remaining burrs, rough spots, or imperfections.

In button rifling, a small carbide plug, or button, with the rifling formed in reverse, is either pushed or pulled through the bore under great pressure. This method irons the rifling into the surface of the bore. In the process, it also evens out minute irregularities in the surface of the bore and the resulting barrel usually has a very smooth bore surface. About the only criticism I have heard about button rifling is that the process causes a springing of the steel as the button is pushed through the bore. The theory suggests that the steel tries to return to its original size and shape after the rifling process is completed. If this theory has any validity, I think any movement of the steel would be microscopic in scope. Since the bullet is much softer than the barrel steel, I would think any results of that would be negligible. Frankly, I think the theory is probably only so many horsefeathers. I have used a few button-rifled barrels and have seen many more used, with perfectly satisfactory results. Shilen uses this method for his barrel production, and his barrels have an excellent reputation.

The third method of rifling is called hammer forging. In this method, a mandrel that contains the rifling in reverse, is placed in the bore. The outside of the barrel is then hammered by a special machine down around the mandrel, which forges the rifling

After a lot of work on a milling machine, this barrel has been converted to an octagonal shape. Much work remains to be done—it must be threaded for the action, chambered for the selected cartridge, and polished to receive the bluing. This work is from the shop of Frank Wells.

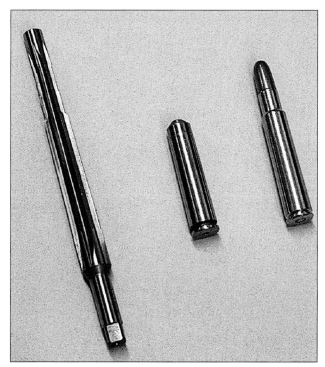

Any maker who does a lot of barrel work will have a substantial investment in chambering reamers and headspace gauges. Some makers I know maintain an inventory of several hundred. On the left is a chambering reamer for the .416 Rigby cartridge and in the middle, a headspace gauge. On the right is a .416 Rigby cartridge.

49

Barrels fabricated from stainless steel are in common use today. Shown here is a heavy barrel varmint model from Dakota Arms. This Model 10 single-shot is chambered for the .22 PPC cartridge and is the personal varmint rifle of the owner of Dakota Arms, Don Allen.

into the bore. As such, hammer forging is quite similar to button rifling, however, hammer forging does have a couple theoretical advantages over button rifling, or cut rifling for that matter. The forging process supposedly work-hardens the surface of the bore and results in a very hard bore surface—much harder that the remainder of the barrel. In addition, the forging process is said to rearrange the molecular structure of the steel, presumably in a positive way. Again, because I am not a metallurgist, I'll have to take an expert's word on the subject.

The F.W. Heym Co., a German rifle manufacturer, did an experiment a couple of years ago that I found very interesting. Heym uses only hammer forging for its barrel production and has one of the largest hammer machines in Europe. It produced two barrels in this experiment. The initial steps in the production process were identical for both barrels. The billets were bored the same, and the newly bored, but unrifled surfaces, were lapped identically. Both barrels were then hammer-forged on the same machinery with the same mandrel. When the two barrels had completed the rifling process, one barrel bore was again lapped and the other was not. The barrels were

then split lengthwise, and the rifled bore of each compared microscopically. As it turned out, the bore on the unlapped barrel was smoother than the barrel that had been lapped after rifling! This finding was both surprising and quite interesting to me.

Each rifling method is capable of producing an exceptionally accurate barrel. Each method can also turn out terrible barrels, incapable of minute-of-buffalo accuracy. Many variables account for why this is so, but perhaps the biggest one is the skill of the barrel maker, regardless of the method used. I am only guessing, but I suspect that the cut rifling method is probably the least expensive technique to produce a barrel, because less costly equipment is required. This fact might well be offset by a greater labor requirement though. I would estimate that the hammer forging method is the most expensive, because very sophisticated and expensive machinery is required. Button rifling is probably somewhere in between. Once the capital investment in equipment is amortized, I suspect it is still more costly to do hammer-forged barrels due to the cost of the necessary mandrels. A separate mandrel is required for each caliber and twist being produced. Of course, the same thing applies to buttons, but a button is presumably cheaper than a mandrel. Both are considerably more expensive than a rifling cutter, but it remains a fact that excellent barrels can be produced from each method. There are also variations of rifling types, such as polygon, micro-groove, and gain twist. Whatever the rifling type, though, they are produced using one of these three methods.

Heavy bull barrels have a reputation of being more accurate than sporter or lightweight models. In general, this is true. The heavier barrels are stiffer and dampen the barrel vibrations much more efficiently. They also weigh a ton, although some makers have made an effort to have the best of both worlds. They mill flutes in the surface of the barrels to lessen the weight. Varmint rifles, bench rest models, and specialty target rifles are usually fitted with stovepipe-sized barrels. Such rifles work fine for their intended purposes, but carrying one of these tack-drivers up the Chugach mountains of Alaska is out of the question. Weight alone rules them out as serious hunting rifles.

Even so, I have seen rifles with barrels so huge that they reminded me of a 105mm howitzer tube, that were not particularly accurate. On the other hand, I have seen pencil-sized barrels that were superbly accurate. All of my personal rifles are hunting rifles, save two. I do have a Ruger No.1 varmint model, chambered for the excellent .22-250 cartridge. I use it for the occasional varmint shooting that I do. I also have an early Winchester Model 52 target rifle. Each of these rifles is fitted with a heavyweight barrel, but the remainder of my rifles have sporter weight barrels.

The three most accurate centerfire rifles I own are a Heym SR-20 7mm Remington magnum, a David Miller Co. custom .270 Winchester, and a Remington Model 700 Light Mountain Rifle, also in the .270 Winchester caliber. Each rifle will deliver three-shot groups measuring under 1/2 inch, provided I do my part. All three rifles are fitted with factory barrels, the Heym and David Miller custom with sporter weight and the Remington with a lightweight barrel no

bigger than my little finger.

The tightest group I have ever shot with any rifle was with the Miller. The three-shot group measured .263 inch center-to-center. A .270 bullet measures .277 inch so that is a very tight group indeed. With the little Remington Light Mountain Rifle, my wife shot a group that measured .357 inch. I haven't been able to get the rifle back from her since. The only modification the Remington received was a new composite stock. The rifle was sent to Garrett Accur-Light, Inc., Ft. Collins, Colorado, for the installation of one of its Ultra-Light stocks. Other than the stock, it is pure factory. The rifle, complete with scope and mounts, weighs slightly over 7 pounds.

There has been much discussion around hunting camps and in the sporting press on the subject of barrel lengths. Some argue that to take advantage of modern magnum calibers using very slow burning powders, a barrel length of at least 26 inches is necessary. That is true, as far as it goes. A general rule of thumb is that about 50 fps of velocity will be lost for each inch the barrel is shortened. The actual losses vary widely, but 50 fps per inch is good enough for discussion here. Yet, there is a price to be paid for the long barrels. Except in wide open country, such rifles are a chore to hunt with. If there is a tree limb or a branch anywhere around, that long barrel will find it. All of my rifles chambered for standard calibers are fitted with 22-inch barrels. My magnum caliber rifles have barrels that are one inch longer. I agree with something that outdoor writer Jon Sundra once wrote to the effect that if the caliber he's using won't get the job done in a 22-inch barrel, he'll change to a caliber that will. That makes sense to me. Even if I have to trade a few feet per second in velocity for a shorter, handier rifle, I will.

Which is the best method of rifling a barrel? I honestly admit that I don't know. I am by no means convinced that one method is superior to the others. I personally use more hammer-forged barrels than any other type, but that wasn't planned. A few makers are still turning out cut-rifled barrels, apparently with

This barrel has had more custom metalsmithing done on it than many entire rifles have. Although not readily apparent in the photo, the quarter-rib, barrel band sling swivel stud, and the barrel band front sight ramp are all milled from the excess steel in the barrel itself. Not seen in the photo is an additional recoil lug integral to the barrel. This superb work was done by Frank Wells. The engraving is by Ken Warren and the photo by Ron Dehn.

great success. Button-rifled barrels are widely available in this country. Obviously, it is far more important how a barrel performs than it is how it was rifled. Unfortunately, performance can only be determined at the range and, by then, it is too late to do anything about it.

I have had perfectly acceptable results with barrels produced by all three methods. I have also had a lemon or two from each type. The best advice is to trust custom makers and let them use what they feel is best. Their reputations are on the line and they will surely use the barrel that they have had the most success with.

Barrel steel technology has also come a long way the past few years. When some high intensity magnum cartridges first came out, the steel used in barrel construction was not up to the task. I am thinking particularly of Winchester's .264 magnum cartridge. It never reached the popularity that it should have for several reasons. One such reason was that it quickly developed a reputation of rapidly eating up barrels. I have read that some users of the caliber had experienced throat erosion so bad that accuracy began to fall off after only a couple hundred shots. I can't vouch for the truth of that because I never experienced the problem. I did own one pre-64 Model 70 chambered for the .264, but didn't shoot it enough to notice any barrel problems.

There is no question, however, that any number of high pressure cartridges

This Colt single-action revolver was converted to a flat-top target model by Bob Snapp. In addition to the flat-top conversion, Snapp also machined the ejector rod housing integral to the barrel, the only one I have ever seen done this way. The engraving is by Frank Hendricks and the grips were fashioned by Steven Dodd Hughes. Photo by Mustafa Bilal.

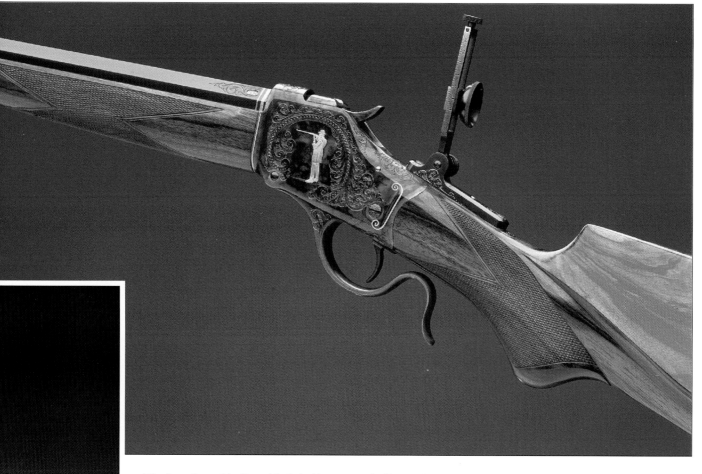

The barrel on this fine rifle is half octagon, half round in shape. The progression between shapes is smoothly accomplished by the use of a "wedding band" transition. Bob Snapp did the metalwork on this rifle. The engraving is by Frank Hendricks and the stock by Steven Dodd Hughes.
Photo by Mustafa Bilal.

commonly used today would be hard on barrels if they could not withstand the extremely high heat and pressures generated. Steel technology has apparently kept up with the developments, though, because it has been a long time since I heard of a barrel erosion complaint.

The latest fad with barrels is a process called Cryogenics. As I understand it, the process involves relieving the stresses in the barrel by subjecting it to temperatures around -300 degrees Fahrenheit for a period of time, usually several hours. It is claimed that this process improves the accuracy and results in longer barrel life. I have never had one of my barrels so treated, so I cannot verify the accuracy of the claims. Several companies have been formed to perform the process though, which is a good indicator that some shooters believe

the process works.

As a final note on barrels, the metalsmiths are beginning to devote extraordinary efforts to barrels these days. They are buying large diameter blanks from the various barrel makers, and, when they get through machining, the resultant barrel is a sight to behold. Barrels that are octagonal or half round/half octagon, integral front sight ramps, rear sight bases, and sling swivel studs, and even integral recoil lugs milled into the oversized blank, are not uncommon these days. The barrel on a rifle offers a lot of metal to play with, and some are really taking advantage of that fact. The recent work I've seen is, by and large, fantastic.

No rifle that is going to be used is better than the quality of its barrel. Many factors contribute to the accuracy potential of a given rifle, and the best barrel in the world won't be very accurate when mated to a poorly bedded stock. Conversely, the most precise and accurately bedded stock will not make a silk purse out of a sow's ear. A precision barrel, whether cut rifled, button rifled, or hammer forged is the key essential element in an accurate rifle.

Chapter 6

Bells and Whistles

One thing among many that sets a custom gun apart from factory products is the number of bells and whistles it has. The list of available options is almost endless. Many features, such as quarter ribs and checkered bolt knobs, have both functional and decorative value. Others, like skeleton gripcaps and buttplates, are purely ornamental.

A rubber recoil pad is simply functional and pretty much standard equipment on many rifles. Few enthusiasts will give one high marks for aesthetic appeal. Its function is, of course, to moderate the effects of recoil on hard kicking rifles. Yet, some makers cover this molded rubber appendage with a film of pigskin. This modification converts a most useful functional feature to one that suffers no loss of function while adding greatly to the aesthetic appeal.

To my eye, a quarter rib really looks sharp on an express-style rifle. They were originally developed, I think, to provide a flat mounting surface on the barrel to attach the rear sight. They work very well for this purpose. These days, though, they are generally more decorative than functional. Most rifles of today are scope-sighted and open sights, if there are any at all, are almost never used. Still, quarter ribs and three-leaf folding express sights seem to go together like ham and eggs. One is rarely seen without the other.

Some, no doubt in an effort to show off just how good they are, will machine a quarter rib from the barrel blank steel. While they are at it, they will gen-

erally also mill a front sight ramp, a sling swivel stud, and sometimes, an extra recoil lug, all from the barrel. To provide enough steel to execute the intricate machining work, the barrel blank they start with approaches the size of a howitzer. Doing the work in this manner is time consuming and requires great skill. The finished product is wonderful, though, and the user never needs to worry about the sights falling off!

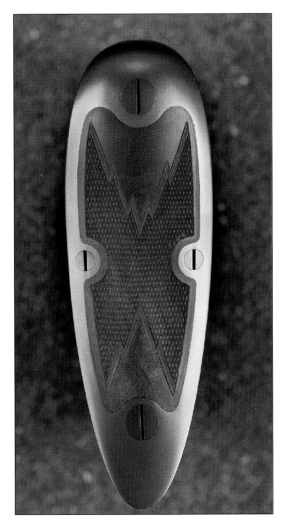

A skeleton buttplate that has been fitted to a custom rifle stock and the wood of the butt checkered. Bruce Russell did this very expert job. Photo by Steven Dodd Hughes.

Some makers fabricate all the parts they need for a project in their shops. Others buy the parts from suppliers and fit them to their project. This barrel band front sight ramp is available to the trade from Brownells.

All of these various sights plus a lot more are available to the trade from New England Custom Gun Service. The folding leaf express-type rear sight can be mated to several types of front sight beads. I like such an express sight mated to the night sight arrangement shown at the top. The night sight has a normal-sized bead with a folding white oversized bead for close work in heavy cover.

Most often, the barrel additions are machined separately and then soldered to the barrel. Properly done, it is almost impossible for the average Joe to detect whether a quarter rib is integral to the barrel or "sweated" on later. I have even seen a couple examples where the quarter rib was fashioned from Damascus steel. One maker also custom made the scope mount bases from the same material. The results were wonderful and certainly different.

Bolt knobs have also become the recipient of functional decoration by makers and artistic decoration by engravers. The functional decoration most often seen on a bolt knob is checkered panels—sometimes one, sometimes two, and sometimes more. The functional advantage in a checkered

The most common rear sight on a heavy caliber magazine rifle is a folding leaf express sight. It is rare to see such a rifle without an express sight. This one is available to the trade from New England Custom Gun Service. It still must be fitted to the rifle and the "V" notches filed in at the range for the specific rifle.

bolt knob is, of course, the non-slip surface that the checkering provides. The decorative aspect deals with the skill with which the checkering is cut.

Sometimes the checkering is cut into a factory bolt knob. That is somewhat more difficult to do because

The bolt knobs of custom rifles are often checkered, both for decorative and functional reasons. The 'smith can checker the factory knob or he can cut it off the bolt and weld on a replacement. Sometimes, they are already checkered, such as the one on the left, or have been investment cast with raised pads to be checkered by the 'smith. The one on the right is of this latter type.

A common modification made to the Model 98 military Mauser action is the addition of a Model 70 type side-swing safety. Some modification to the original safety is necessary if a scope is to be mounted on the finished rifle. Often, the original cocking piece is removed and replaced with a new one, including the new safety. This one is produced by Jim Wisner.

A very nice custom touch for shotguns and light recoiling rifles is a skeleton buttplate. A buttplate like this one is inletted into the butt of the stock and the protruding wood of the butt is most often checkered. Many early high-grade shotguns, such as the Parker, came from the factory fitted with skeleton buttplates.

the top of the checkered diamonds cut into the steel are at the same height as the surrounding material. Steel checkering files can be used at the center of the panels, but the edges are usually cut with engraving tools. A maker can also weld on a bolt handle with an oversized knob. This provides enough excess material to file away some steel and leaves raised "pads" into which the panels are checkered. Using raised pads permits doing much of the checkering with a metal checkering file, reducing the need for engraving tools. Bolt handles that have the raised panels cast into the knobs are available on the market, as are bolt handles with the checkering already finished.

An assortment of custom touches available from Dakota Arms: A Dakota rifle customer can order any of these as optional features on his rifle. Dakota also offers this hardware to the trade.

Some makers are content to install readily available scope mount bases from one of the various manufacturers and others are not. One that I know of, the David Miller Company, makes its own complete mount, including rings. A few others make their own bases for factory rings. Some will purchase factory bases and rings and modify them to suit their needs.

Stockmakers lavish a number of options on their work as well. Gripcaps can be provided in a number of shapes and configurations. The days of a simple horn gripcap are long since past—today most are from steel, either solid or with one of various designs of skeleton cutouts. The same is true of buttplates and the same general selections are available. I think a matching skeleton gripcap and buttplate, with precise checkering in the skeleton cutouts, makes for a beautiful custom stock. If the stock is to be used for hunting, however, I would think twice about having such a buttplate installed. They are too damage prone for my hunting rifles. For a fine custom shotgun, a skeleton buttplate works fine, though.

Factory magazine box/triggerguard combinations often leave much to be desired aesthetically. Many military models are stamped metal and some commercial models are not very stylish. Usually, the original hardware is either modified or replaced. Some metalsmiths mill their own bottom metal in their shops. Most commonly, they buy a replacement from a specialist. Jim Wisner, Ted Blackburn, and Dakota Arms all offer finished replacements to the trade. This one is from Wisner.

A few variations on replaceable gripcaps offered by New England Custom Gun Service: These gripcaps come in two pieces, a base and the cap itself. The base is inletted into the stock and the cap can then be changed as desired.

The epitome of bells and whistles are these accessories provided with the Safari Club International Simba-M'Bogo rifle by maker Frank Wells. The rifle, including the accessories, sold at auction for $105,000. Photo by Ron Dehn.

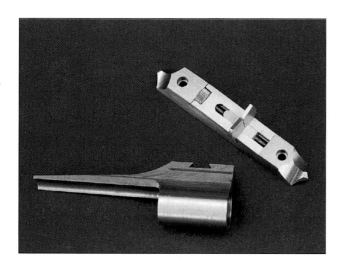

Sights come in all sizes and types: Shown here is a barrel band front sight ramp and a magnum Model 70 type adjustable rear sight. Both are available from Jim Wisner.

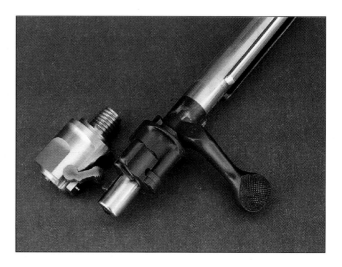

On the right is a magnum Mauser bolt with the original cocking piece/safety combination. On the left is a replacement which features a Model 70 type side-swing safety.

A variation of the skeleton buttplate that was somewhat popular at one time was heel and toe caps. Once again, though, they are more suitable for a fine custom shotgun than they are rifles—at least I think they are. Graceful steel heel and toe caps, perhaps scroll engraved, along with the end grain of the stock in between nicely checkered, sure make for an elegant shotgun stock.

Although I may be chastised for doing so, I have chosen to include checkering under the category of bells and whistles. Admittedly, many checkering jobs should not be so categorized—a quality checkering job is properly a component part of any custom stock. It is only when the checkerer goes to overly elaborate patterns that it, I believe, changes categories. I am a sucker for precisely cut checkering. Nothing in my view, with the possible exception of a magnificent stick of wood, is more important in a fine custom stock than an expertly cut checkering pattern.

It should be cut fine enough to look good, yet not so fine as to lose its functional purpose. For me, that means about 26 lines per inch. The pattern used, whether a traditional point pattern or my favored fleur-de-lis, should provide enough coverage to be both functional and decorative, but not so much as to be overpowering.

Unfortunately, some craftspeople seem to theorize that if some checkering is good, more is better. To showcase their checkering skills, they use overly large patterns with lots of ribbons, curlicues, and didos. They then tend to use checkering so fine that it is almost slick to the touch. I have done a fair amount of checkering myself and can attest first-hand to the difficulty involved in doing elaborate patterns. Even a fairly simple pattern will sometimes make a monk change religions. Even so, I think that overly complex patterns detract from rather than enhance a fine stock. If the checkering pattern is the first thing

noticed on the gun, then it is probably overdone.

Any custom gun worth its salt is deserving of a custom housing as well. This can vary from simply a finely crafted leather gun case turned out by a quality saddle shop, to a British style oak-and-leather-type trunk. Casemaker Marvin Huey has made a career making this latter type housing. Starting with a wooden box, Marvin custom fits the firearm and any desired accessories into the box, then covers the inside with either felt or ultrasuede. Once that is done, he then covers the exterior of the case in flawless cowhide. If desired, he can also provide a canvas overcase to protect the fine leather. His cases are superb and exhibit a quality fitting to enhance an equal quality custom gun.

A newcomer to the custom case business is Jim Hasson. Hasson specializes in making the highest quality pistol cases I have seen. His contrasting wood inlay work is so good that it has to be seen to be appreciated. Working with several different exotic woods, he can do most anything a customer desires. His cases are intended to be display cases only, not transport protection. Huey's work, on the other hand, serves both roles very well although anyone who puts one in the back of a pickup deserves to be tarred and feathered.

Of course, that is what the custom business is all about. If a given client wants checkering from buttplate to forend on a gun, so be it. If nothing but a $2,000 oak-and-leather trunk will satisfy his or her idea of pickup transport, that's fine. It's his or her money. So it is with all the bells and whistles. The selection is vast. A quick look through the Brownells catalog will provide a good overview of readily available items and prices for the various items. These prices do not, of course, include installation. That would be a subject of discussion between the maker and the client.

Chapter 7

Sights and Sight Mounts

his chapter will concentrate mostly on sighting arrangements for custom rifles. Although some custom handguns, particularly those crafted for the popular shooting competitions of today, are outfitted with rather exotic sights, most haven't changed in a century. Shotguns are in the same category. About the only difference in scattergun sights is whether the barrel has but one bead or two!

No, it is the rifle that has motivated the development of a wide variety of sighting arrangements. Of course, that makes perfectly good sense. Both handguns and shotguns are, at best, short-range firearms. Fifty yards is a very long shot with either and most are shorter. At such "whites of the eyes" ranges, no high tech developments for sighting are required. Most scattergunners could make do quite nicely with no sights at all! Rifles, on the other hand, are commonly used in hunting situations at ranges out to a few hundred yards. Varmint shooters push the envelope even farther. Some competitive events for rifle shooters even feature thousand yard matches. With a hunting rifle, the sights can make the

difference between a clean kill and a miss, or even worse, a wounded animal. In competitive matches, it can determine the winners and losers.

Before I am taken to task by handgun hunters, I am aware that using a handgun for hunting is becoming more and more popular. In that particular usage, the sighting arrangements on a hunting handgun are every bit as important as on a rifle. In fact, the handguns used for the sport are, by and large, essentially handheld rifles with short barrels. Some of them are exceptionally accurate and in the hands of an experienced shooter, very effective. Still, they are the exception rather than the rule.

Up until about the time WWII kicked off, rifles were fitted with two types of sights. There were several variations, but in principle, there were only two types. By far the most common was a bead front sight paired with a notched rear sight—probably 95 percent or so were fitted with this type. Many of the rear sights were adjustable for elevation and the notches took many shapes. There were simple "V" notches, "U" notches, square notches, and about every other

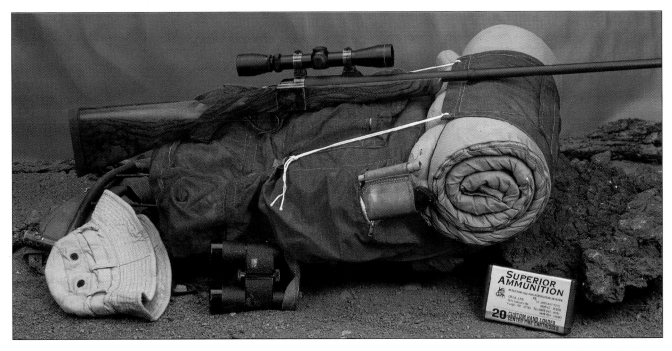

The author's Dakota Model 10 single-shot chambered for the 7mm Dakota cartridge. It is fitted with a Leupold scope in Dave Talley mounts. The rings, along with the action, were beautifully case colored by Doug Turnbull.

This John Rigby .375 H&H is fitted with open sights only. The rear sight is an express-type sight with one standing and two folding leaves for different ranges. The front sight is a simple bead.

shape one could come up with. The front sight blades were also varied from the most common bead to a flat post. I have also seen them sharpened to a point, rounded, and on one odd rifle I can recall, the front sight was triangular in shape!

The second type occasionally encountered was one of several forms of the peep sight. Here, we are referring to the rear sight only because the front remained the same. The peep sights varied in complexity from a very simple bar with a hole through it and very little adjustments to micrometer precise adjustments in both windage and elevation. The eyepieces were also adjustable in some models. Most models permitted the eyepieces to be changed with replacements that provided either smaller or larger holes. Although far less common than the standard open sights, peep sights are very effective by comparison.

The English modified the open sight arrangement somewhat for their dangerous game rifles. World renowned for their double rifles, most were fitted with what we now call express sights for a rear sight and a bead front with a folding night sight insert. The folding bead was usually quite large in diameter and faced with ivory. The theory was that the smaller bead sight would be used for more precise shooting in normal light but in fading light or in dense cover, the night sight could be popped up for better visibility. The rear sight generally featured a solid standing leaf sighted for about 50 yards and one or more folding leaves sighted for 100, 200, and so on.

These days, though, with a couple exceptions, any sighting arrangement other than a scope is seldom seen. Scopes of all types and magnifications are available on the market with models adequate for almost any use and in all price ranges. About the only exceptions to the scope takeover is on heavy caliber dangerous game rifles, rifles tailored for competition where scopes are not allowed, and rifles intended for heavy cover, short-range hunting situations, primarily eastern whitetail hunting. For the most part, scopes are it. The chance of encountering a hunter in the field armed with a rifle that is not scope-sighted is pretty remote these days. Many custom rifles and not an inconsequential number of factory models are delivered with no sights at all.

I personally like the looks of a rifle with no additional sights other that a scope. I think they have a cleaner look about them. Still, there is a group of shooters that insists on fixed sights in addition to the scope. Most in that category have had a bad experience with their scopes. A pal of mine hunts Africa often and he uses but one rifle. The rifle is a .375 H&H and has both factory open sights as well as a premium scope in EAW quick detachable mounts.

On one trip, as he was unpacking his gear in camp after the several thousand mile trip, he unpacked his rifle for a quick check at the camp's makeshift range. When he looked through the scope, the reticule was missing! It was still in the tube somewhere, but not

An express-type rear sight as it comes from the shop of Gary Stiles: This particular rifle is a takedown with two sets of barrels. It was stocked by Bill Simmen. Photo by Mark Ross, courtesy of GUNS magazine.

where it was supposed to be. He removed the scope and hunted very successfully for a couple weeks using only the open sights. He won't have a rifle that is not equipped with additional sights.

Early scope models were developed primarily by the Germans. Compared to what is available today, they were pretty frightful affairs. They were fragile, fogged every time the weather changed, and cost an arm and a leg to buy. The mounts available to attach them to the rifle were equally inadequate. It was a good beginning, but had a long way to go. Most American hunters either couldn't afford one or didn't trust them, so they weren't very popular. There was justification in both reasons for not owning one.

Scopes floundered along rather aimlessly until Bill Weaver came onto the scene. Weaver developed a good scope that was reliable, relatively sturdy, and, while not cheap, was within the financial reach of most hunters. He also developed a reliable, uncomplicated, and inexpensive mount to attach the scope to one's rifle. After these events, all other sighting systems slowly fell by the wayside.

These days, it is rare to encounter a rifle in the field that is not scope-mounted. Even in those areas that require shotguns with slugs for deer hunting, more and more are showing up with scopes. The same is true with blackpowder guns. Except for the guys who run around clad in buckskins toting a flintlock, scopes are becoming the sights of choice on more modern blackpowder models.

Initially, all the available scopes were fixed power models of low magnification. Most were in the range of 1.5X up to 4X. As the optical scope technology advanced, more powerful models came onto the scene. It didn't take long for the 4X and 6X models to

Germany's solution to a quick detachable mount is this claw mounting system. This mounting system is most often encountered on combination guns. It works, but it is very expensive and somewhat fragile. More modern systems such as those by EAW are less expensive and much more sturdy.

A barrel band front sight ramp and hood as done by Gary Stiles. Not only is this arrangement attractive, but it is also very functional. Photo by Mark Ross, courtesy of GUNS magazine.

This custom Model 70 by Gary Goudy features commercially available scope mounts that have been modified for this rifle. Two-piece bases such as these are amply strong and do the job very well.

This custom Model 52 Winchester required a set of mount bases that were custom machined specifically for this rifle. They were further machined to accept commercially available rings. The exquisite rifle is from the shop of Gary Goudy.

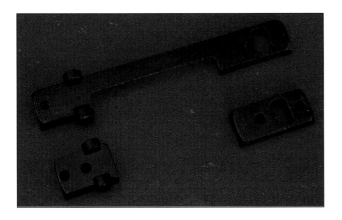

Redfield one-piece and two-piece bases have been around for a long time and I suspect they will be around for a lot longer. They are simple, easy to install, strong, and relatively inexpensive.

edge out the lower power models in popularity. Eyes got older and weaker, and more magnification became the norm.

Finally, someone came up with the idea of developing a scope that could be varied in magnification as the situation demanded. At the mere twist of a ring on the scope tube, the magnification could be changed to accommodate long shots, close in shots, and everything in between. In theory, that sounded like the best of both worlds and now the variable scope is the scope of choice. Fixed power scopes are slowly fading away in popularity.

Variable scopes initially had a number of bugs that had to be corrected. Early models were more fragile, much more prone to leakage and fogging, and with all the inside moving parts, more apt to develop mechanical problems. A fair number of the outdoor press recommended against them for these reasons. Still, the concept was a good one and the shooting public continued to demand variables over fixed power models. The scope manufacturers responded by improving variables to the point where they are, practically speaking, every bit as durable as fixed power models.

I must admit that most of my scopes are also variable models. It has been my experience, though, that in my case as well as almost all of my hunting pals, variables are not used in practice according to the theory. While the capability is there to alter the magnification of the scope according to the situation, most don't use them that way. If the scope on my rifle happens to be a 2X to 7X variable, it is invariably set at 7X all the time. Of course, I could change it to another magnification if I wanted to, but in practice, I don't. Neither does anyone else I know. I guess that just knowing that we could change them if we wanted to is justification enough for most users.

Reticules have come a long way as well. Early on, just about every manufacturer had a series of special reticules for their scopes. They varied in complexity from a simple dot to just about everything the maker

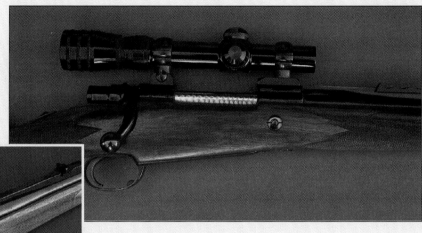

Shown here is the Redfield two-piece base system on the author's .375 H&H. It is a good, strong system and works well even on large calibers.

Redfield one-piece and two-piece bases have been around for a long time and I suspect they will be around for a lot longer. They are simple, easy to install, strong, and relatively inexpensive.

could cram into the tube. The Germans turned out some real doozies. Of particular complexity were some of the rangefinding schemes. In many cases the user had to be a rocket scientist and carry a calculator to figure out how to use them. Most of that has gone the way of the dodo bird, though. In American scopes of today, some form of the duplex reticule is far and away the most popular. There are variations in design between manufacturers, but all have four crosswires that are heavier at the perimeter that taper to a fine crosswire at the center. It is a very good reticule for hunting and most scopes are so equipped these days. The Europeans still like reticules that are more complex, but even they offer a duplex style reticule for the American market.

There is a wide range of scopes on the market in the $200 to $400 range. They are all good instruments that work well and do the job they were intended to do—they offer good value for their cost. In the past few years, several European manufacturers have made inroads into the American market with premium quality (and price) scopes. Optically, most of them are superior to most American models. They are, in general, clearer and brighter and will often add a good hour to the hunters day. That hour is added at the most productive hunting times—an additional half hour in the morning and another at dark. This is a great advantage, but it is achieved at greatly increased cost; some are two to three times the cost of

an equivalent American model.

Obviously, there are many hunters out there who are willing to come up with the added cash to buy one, because the European models are selling well. This fact has not gone unnoticed by the American competition. Some manufacturers, most notably Leupold, have come out with a European line of scopes to compete. How well they will be accepted by the shooting public remains to be seen.

Scopes are very durable these days and almost all are sealed against moisture. No scope, however, is more durable than its mounting system. Fortunately, mounts these days are universally strong and effective. Many different makes and models are on the market, but most fall into the category of two-piece base or one-piece base bridge mounts. They vary in price from perhaps $30 to $100, or more. Properly installed, they all seem to work well.

A few mounting systems have appeared on the market as quick detachable mounts. They tout the ability to quickly remove the scope and then remount it, with no loss of zero. Some of the early side mounts worked well, but they are seldom seen anymore. Most top mount models that I have seen, though, were not very accurate in returning to zero. The one that I have used most, and if properly adjusted it does return to zero, is the EAW mount. Using this mount, all that is necessary to remove the scope is to unlatch it at the rear mount with a lever and swing the scope

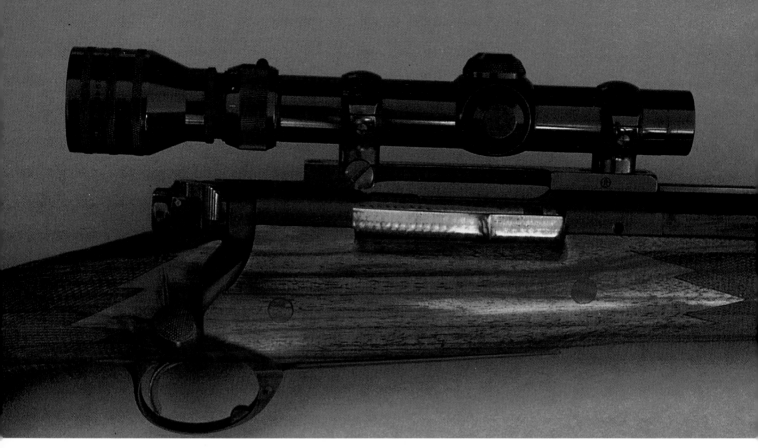

Redfield also offers a one-piece mount base, such as this one on the author's custom Model 70 .375 H&H magnum. Theoretically, the one-piece base is stronger than the two-piece model. In practice, though, both are amply strong and the two-piece model is easier to load ammo into the magazine.

Traditional German claw mounts are good, but very expensive. Repeated removal of the scope will cause the feet to wear unless they are properly hardened. If this happens, the scope will, in time, get sloppy and not return to zero. Properly done, though, it works very well and will last a long time.

These mounts from Dave Talley are very popular with custom makers these days and with good reason. They are excellent mounts, very sturdy, and attractive on a fine custom rifle.

One of the best quick detachable mounts available is that from EAW. Properly adjusted, these mounts permit the removal and reattachment of the scope as often as necessary without loss of zero.

This Heym SR-20 .375 H&H was modified by the author to be his "knock around" big bore. It features a low magnification scope mounted in EAW quick detachable mounts. It is also equipped with an adjustable rear sight from Jim Wisner and a night sight front bead. The stock is a McMillan fiberglass model to withstand rough usage. It may not be pretty, but it is dependable in almost any circumstance.

to the front. It can be removed and remounted in a second or two. The down side is that they cost about twice as much as a top end fixed mount. They do work, though.

There is no question that scopes are the sights of choice these days. The next question is, where do we go from here? I suspect the next development will be the addition of compact laser rangefinders within the scope. Swarovski already has one model with this feature, but it certainly isn't compact. The state of the art hasn't miniaturized the rangefinder to the point where it can be considered practical yet. In addition, the cost is still prohibitive. Even so, I believe it will happen in the next few years. It would be a wonderful development because

most hunters are poor at estimating range. The technology is there, but it is just a matter of refinement.

I still remember my first calculator. I paid $99.95 for it on a special buy sale. It was the size of a box of .270 ammo and would add, subtract, multiply, divide, and it performed a couple other functions. Today, a similar calculator is the size of a credit card and costs $1.99, if that. Many places give them away as promotional items. Hopefully, laser rangefinders will progress similarly, but, if they do, there is one downside. Those interesting tall tales of 600-yard shots told around the campfire will disappear—maybe!

Chapter 8

Engraving, Carving, and Inlays

At about the time Adam started chasing Eve around the apple tree in Eden, humans acquired a craving to decorate things. If they could find nothing else to satisfy this primeval urge, they decorated themselves. We sometimes think of tattooing as a modern fantasy, but it isn't. Prehistoric mortals cut themselves open with flint knives and rubbed all sorts of pigmented concoctions into the resulting gashes. When healed, provided the recipient didn't die of infection, the resulting tinted scars made the bearer different from everyone else. Keeping up with the Joneses was both painful and risky in those days.

Ken Warren adorned the buttplate of this Frank Wells rifle with scroll and gold inlay. Crafted for Safari Club International, the rifle sold at auction for $105,000. Photo by Ron Dehn.

As weaponry evolved, it was quite natural that one's club, stone hatchet, lance, sword, bow, and later firearm, would become the recipient of ornamentation. That trend continues to this day. Some of the work being done today on modern firearms is so good that it is mind-boggling, but alas, some that I have seen is also terrible.

Good engraving, or bad for that matter, is totally a result of individual talent or lack thereof. The tools used are simple, relatively inexpensive, and play little role in the quality of the finished product. It is the wielding of these simple tools that creates a masterpiece or a monstrosity, not the tool itself. Our best engravers could turn out works of art using ground down screwdrivers as gravers.

There are several different styles of engraving. Styling varies from deeply chiseled, bas-relief engraving associated with the Germanic school of artisans, to delicate *bulino* engraving executed to perfection by the best of the Italian engravers. Germanic engraving is bold, eye catching, and can be appreciated from a substantial distance. On the other hand, *bulino* engraving by such masters as Fracassi and Galeazzi, requires a magnifying glass to fully appreciate the magnificence of the work.

English engraving is famous for delicate scrollwork, often with a floral design. It seems to me that cutting the tiny scrolls, one after the other, would drive a Baptist preacher to drink. The Brits seem to thrive on it, though. So do the Italians. German, Austrian, or Belgian engravers would head for the nearest moonshine still if they had to execute that style of engraving very often.

American engravers, typical of practically everything else in American society, execute patterns that run the gamut of styling. I have seen engraving done by American artisans that rivaled the best of the Italian *bulino* styling, yet on the very next table were examples of deep, bas-relief styling that could not be distinguished from Germanic styling.

Generally, the styling executed by individual engravers depends on the styling favored by either their teachers, or if self-trained, the styling executed by their idols. Eventually, though, most artisans develop their own variations of a style. If successful in their pursuits of excellence, individual variations

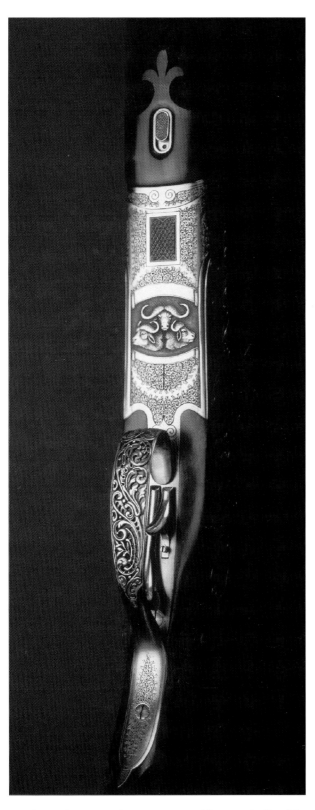

Perhaps the most elegant Heym rifle ever built, this sidelock double rifle was built for Safari Club International. German Master Engraver Erich Boessler did the engraving. The rifle was the Buffalo Rifle in a series of five, hence the buffalo theme in the engraving. Boessler also did the magnificent filigree work on the triggerguard. Photo courtesy of F.W. Heym.

usually evolve to such a degree that the work can be recognized immediately. A good example is the craftsmanship of Master Engraver Lynton McKenzie. The way he executes his scrollwork, his trademark engraving so to speak, is instantly recognizable. This is true for practically all engravers at the top of their profession.

As mentioned earlier, the tools of the trade are simple and mostly inexpensive. The most expensive item on an engraver's bench is normally a good vise. Most, but not all engravers, use some form of a ball vise, which, according to the latest Brownells catalog, runs about $500. Unless the engraver uses one of the power tools such as the Gravermeister, a good vise represents one's largest shop investment. Few engravers I know personally use power equipment. Most rely on a chasing hammer instead.

When I first traveled to Germany in 1961, courtesy of the US Army, I had a few goals in mind, the most important of which was to find a good engraver to decorate a few of my personal firearms. Unfortunately, I didn't have success on that trip. I came back home in 1964 with a new bride and a son on the way, but not a single engraved firearm.

Five years later, Uncle Sam decided to send me back to the old country for a second tour. This time, however, I had the good fortune to locate a master engraver to embellish some of my guns. As it turned out, I was already familiar with his artistry, but didn't even know his name. I had seen examples of his work on the covers and in stories published in our various gun magazines, but unfortunately, credit for the work was given to the company that had commissioned the engraving, not to the engraver. The engraver's name was not even mentioned. The master engraver I am referring to, Erich Boessler, lives and works in Muennerstadt, a small German town not far from the pre-war gunmaking center of Suhl. Muennerstadt is located on the western side of what used to be the Iron Curtain. Suhl is on the eastern side of that former divide. Boessler, a native of the Suhl area, sneaked across the border as a young man and went to work as an engraver for the Heym factory. Heym had preceded him in escaping to the West.

After a few years as one of several factory engravers, Boessler earned his certificate as a master engraver and struck out on his own. He continued to work with Heym on special projects, but also accepted commissions from other factories, in addition to private clients. Besides his engraving, he also tutored apprentice engravers and helped them to learn the craft. He likewise usually had at least one finished engraver in his shop who was studying to become a master engraver. When I first met Boessler, one other engraver worked in his shop, Rolf Peter. Peter was studying to earn his master's certificate under Boessler's tutelage.

Boessler is one of the most versatile engravers I have ever known. While he is perhaps at his best when doing traditional Germanic-style engraving, he is equally proficient when cutting English scroll or Italian-style banknote, or *bulino*, engraving. If there is any form of engraving that he cannot do well, I haven't come across it.

Boessler did much work for me and, over the years, we became close friends. I observed the master at work in his shop for many hours. Many fine engravers, who were studying for their coveted certificate that identified them as master engravers, passed through his shop. All I know who studied under him have gone on to become outstanding engravers in their own rights. He is now retired and only accepts commissions that he wants to execute and if he has no time limits on completing the job.

Another German master engraver, who is a good friend, is Claus Willig from Schweinfurt. I first met Willig through his American agent, Dietrich Apel. Apel owned Paul Jaeger, Inc. at the time and during a visit to Germany, I stopped in on Willig for a visit. Although he has done beautiful work for years, I think he is doing the very best work of his career right now.

Yet another engraver friend is Lynton McKenzie. McKenzie's work has been publicized for years and he is among the very best at his art. His style is dis-

tinctive and to a knowledgeable enthusiast, his work is instantly recognizable.

Another American engraver I recently met whose talent is among the most advanced that I have seen is Winston Churchill. No, he is not the late British Prime Minister, and I doubt that he is even remotely related. He is instead a native New Englander. I have seen several examples of Churchill's artistry, and if anyone is better at scratching in steel, I have yet to see it.

A pal of mine who is doing excellent work is Ken Warren of Wenatchee, Washington. Warren works primarily in the Germanic style and he is particularly adept at doing the deeply chiseled, high relief engraving.

Another American engraver doing outstanding work is Ron Smith. I first met Smith when I presented the *GUNS* magazine first annual Award of Excellence at the 1995 combined Firearms Engravers Guild of America/American Custom Gunmakers Guild annual show. The winning entry in the competition was a wonderful single shot rifle built on a Hagn action by Maurice Ottmar. Smith executed the extraordinary engraving on the rifle. He is located in Ft. Worth, Texas, and his work is so good that I must have been under an Arizona rock somewhere for not recognizing his talents earlier.

A dear friend of mine had a wonderful custom rifle built up by the late Jules LaBantchni of Santa

Monica, California. The Mauser action .338 Winchester magnum was absolutely exquisite. To top off the project, my pal sent the rifle to Robert Swartley, a California engraver, with a sketch detailing how he wanted it engraved. Swartley executed the pattern wonderfully. A few years after the project was completed, my friend passed away at an all too young age. He bequeathed the rifle to me in his will. That was the only sample of Swartley's work that I have ever owned, but I have seen several other exam-

Virginian Lisa Tomlin did the lovely engraving on this John Bolliger Signature Series custom rifle. The rifle is chambered for the .416 Remington cartridge, hence the Cape buffalo scene on the floorplate. Photo courtesy of John Bolliger.

ples. His engraving style is very distinctive and always executed to perfection.

Engraving is not solely a male bastion, either. One lady who is doing superb work is Lisa Tomlin of Huddleston, Virginia. Tomlin's most recent major project was the engraving on the latest Safari Club International rifle. Built by gunmaker John Bolliger of Mountain Riflery, the Elephant Rifle was the final gun in SCI's latest five year, five rifle project. This magnificent rifle was adorned by Tomlin's equally splendid engraving.

Mentioning engravers by name in a piece such as this, is always fraught with peril. Space doesn't permit mentioning them all and those omitted are often offended. I intend no such slight. I have cited only those engravers whose work I am personally well acquainted with. Sam Welch, Ben Shostle, Terry Wallace, Bob Evans, Marty Rabeno, Angelo Bee, Bryan Bridges, Mike Dubber, Ray Viramontez, Frank Hendricks, and many others, all execute outstanding work.

So far, I haven't mentioned any engravers from Austria, Belgium, England, or Italy. Here again, I mean no offense by the omission. I have seen little of their work personally, although I have seen much of their artistry via published photos. I will mention a few that I know only by reputation.

The best of the Belgian engravers was, I believe, the late Louis Vrancken. Vrancken was, as I understand it, the chief engraver for the F.N. factory for many years. I believe that he also headed the Belgian engraving school. Examples of his engraving that I have seen publicized, were superb.

The great Austrian engraver, the late Albin Obiltschnig, was highly publicized in this country until his death. His Germanic-style engraving was very well done. Another Obiltschnig, Hans by name, is also doing wonderful Germanic-style engraving. I assume that the younger Obiltschnig is a relative of Albin, perhaps even his son. Another Austrian engraver that made quite a splash for awhile in this country was Franz Marktl. I have heard nothing about him in recent years and don't know if he is still in the business. His work though, was first rate.

Although I am sure that there are many fine English engravers, I personally know of but two. Ken Hunt has engraved for most of the prestigious English makers and his talent has often been publicized here. From the photos that I have seen of his work, it is superb. Another whose exquisite artistry I became acquainted with when doing a story on Symes & Wright, is Rashid el Hadi. At the time he was the chief engraver for that company. His work is magnificent. He is a young man who will be around for many years to come.

There are also many wonderful Italian engravers.

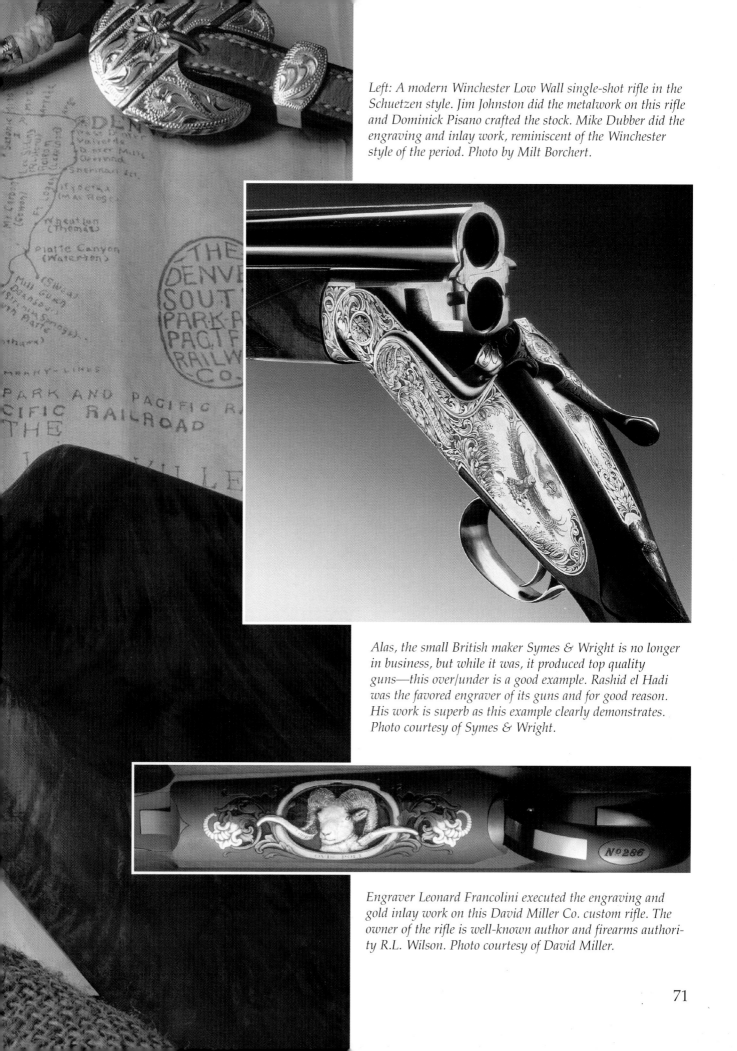

Left: A modern Winchester Low Wall single-shot rifle in the Schuetzen style. Jim Johnston did the metalwork on this rifle and Dominick Pisano crafted the stock. Mike Dubber did the engraving and inlay work, reminiscent of the Winchester style of the period. Photo by Milt Borchert.

Alas, the small British maker Symes & Wright is no longer in business, but while it was, it produced top quality guns—this over/under is a good example. Rashid el Hadi was the favored engraver of its guns and for good reason. His work is superb as this example clearly demonstrates. Photo courtesy of Symes & Wright.

Engraver Leonard Francolini executed the engraving and gold inlay work on this David Miller Co. custom rifle. The owner of the rifle is well-known author and firearms authority R.L. Wilson. Photo courtesy of David Miller.

71

Engraver Eric Gold adorned this Hughes-Fox double with light coverage but exquisitely done scrollwork. Steven Dodd Hughes completely rebuilds Fox doubles and turns them into modern classic game guns. The Gold engraving complements the guns wonderfully. Photo by Steven Dodd Hughes.

Two who are particularly outstanding are Firmo Fracassi and Angelo Galeazzi. These two engravers have long since perfected the art of *bulino* engraving. This wonderfully delicate style of engraving is so ethereal, that a magnifying glass is required to fully appreciate it. Other Italian engravers at the top of their profession are Gianfranco Pedersoli, Fausto Galeazzi, Claudio Tomasoni, and Aldo Rizzini.

No matter what country an engraver happens to call home, artistic talent and the ability to convey that artistry to steel knows no nationality. An excellent way to study engravers and engraving styles is to obtain a copy of one or more books on the subject. While books on this topic are not as commonly seen as those on many other subjects, several have been printed. One of the best that I know of was written by an Italian, the late gunmaker Mario Abbiatico. The title of the book is simply *Modern Firearm Engravings*. This book, printed in English, was copyrighted in

Engraver Terry Theis did the engraving and inlay work on this floorplate of a Wayne Baker custom rifle. Theis, a Texan, executed a rather unusual southwestern-style pattern by inlaying prickly pear cactus into the scene. Photo by Marc Bennett.

72

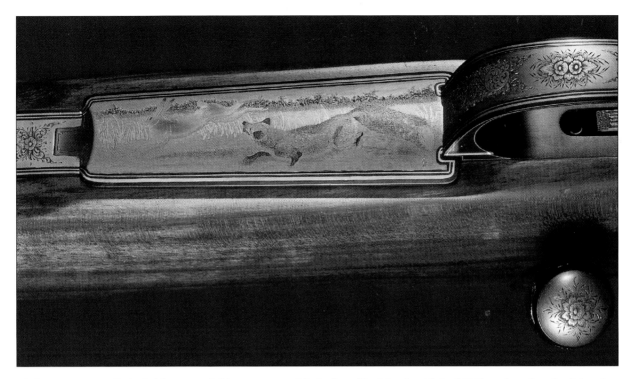

Arizona engraver Eric Gold executed this scene on a .22 rimfire rifle. Metalsmith Jack Belk and stockmaker Maurice Ottmar built the rifle in the style of a British Express rifle, but scaled down in keeping with appropriate dimensions for the .22 long rifle cartridge. Gold's fox and hare scene on the floorplate is also in keeping with the chambering. Photo by Steven Dodd Hughes.

Factory engraving from Dakota Arms: The Dakota shotgun is a relatively new product from the well-known rifle company. This model, the Legend, is the top-of-the-line model.

1980. In 1982, an expanded version of the same tome was printed in Italian, but, to my knowledge, was not published in English. It is entitled *L'incisione delle Armi Sportive*.

Whether either is still in print or not, I cannot say. Both books are beautifully illustrated and have excellent references. It might be necessary to cruise used bookstores or subscribe to listings from sporting book dealers to find a copy. If a copy can be found, though, it is well worth the effort. Most of the engraving pictured in the books was done by Italian engravers, but it also features illustrations of engraving from Germany, Austria, Belgium, Great Britain, and the USA. There are also short biographical sketches on many of the individual engravers.

Another excellent book on the subject is *American Engravers* by C. Roger Bleile. Although it is a bit dated

as well, also copyrighted in 1980, it is nevertheless very useful. Much of the information it contains is surely obsolete, but many of the featured engravers are still going strong. Unfortunately the book is out of print and used bookstores or specialty dealers are probably the only sources of a copy. I lucked out and found my copy in a small town used bookstore.

I think the book is especially useful in that the photography is very good. I think it points out examples in excellent detail of really good engraving, as well as examples that are pretty bad. There seems to be only two qualities of engraving, super good and terrible. Middle-of-the-road engraving just doesn't seem to exist.

I have been told about a new book from author R.L. Wilson called, I think, *Steel Canvas*. I haven't personally seen a copy yet, but I am told that it is splen-

A fan commissioned this Government Model .45 for presentation to General Norman Schwarzkopf. The unusual engraving depicts various aspects of the General's military career. Mike Dubber, the engraver, personally presented the piece to the General. Photo by Milt Borchert.

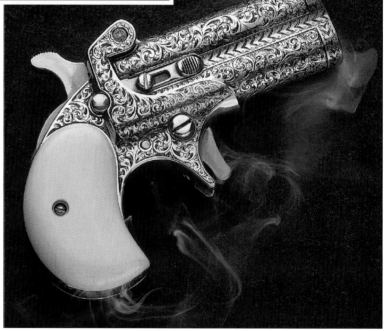

A modern version of a classic Derringer: This one is constructed from stainless steel and is chambered for the .357 magnum pistol round. Engraver Ralph Ingle fully decorated the piece with German floral scroll in high relief, with a black background. It is also adorned with custom fitted ivory grips. Photo courtesy of Ralph Ingle.

did. Knowing the quality of the other books from Wilson, I'm sure that it is superb, and I can hardly wait to get my hands on a copy.

A few periodicals, most notably *GUNS* magazine, also provide editorial coverage of engraving and engravers. Many issues of *GUNS* feature outstanding photography of engraved firearms. Some of the other monthly publications occasionally publish material on engraving as well. The annual issue of *Gun Digest* customarily contains a section called "Art of the Engraver." Most issues of this classic publication feature three or four full pages of engraving photography.

Engraving preferences, like painting and sculpting, are subject to personal whims and taste. Some art connoisseurs are so impressed that they go into a trance when viewing the works of van Gogh, Picasso, or Miro. Others snort and fume, finding their work ghastly. The old adage "different strokes for different folks" applies to engraving as well as all other art forms. Fortunately, there are enough engravers around to satisfy practically any taste.

An engraving job starts with the design of the pattern. Sometimes, engravers "doodle" directly on the steel until they are satisfied with the design. In other cases, an elaborate drawing is created and sent to the client for approval. One thing is for sure—if engravers cannot draw an acceptable design on paper, they certainly cannot be expected to satisfactorily cut such a pattern into the steel.

Once the design is completed, the engraver begins to cut the pattern into the steel of the piece being engraved. He or she will usually do this by using one of two methods. One method is to use a chasing hammer for power and guide the graver around the pattern while tapping on it with the hammer. A second

This modern Sharps rifle is from Shiloh Sharps and is engraved by Montana artist Bill Gamradt. Gamradt has engraved a number of the reproduction Sharps Long Range Express rifles. The photo is by the engraver.

method is to use only a hand graver. Practically all Germanic-style engravers use the chasing hammer method. The more delicate *bulino*-style engraving relies primarily on the hand graver and muscle power alone. On many jobs, and perhaps most, both methods will be employed.

Some engravers have replaced the chasing hammer with a power tool, such as the Gravermeister. Whether using a simple hammer or a technologically advanced power tool, though, the process is the same. Some engravers believe that using the power tool speeds up their work while others stay with the chasing hammer.

The background around scrollwork is frequently stippled to provide a degree of depth to the pattern. Most engravers pay scant attention to the preciseness of the stippling. In their view, it is simply a background and not a major contributor to the overall quality of the engraving. One exception to this philosophy is the artistry of Lynton McKenzie. McKenzie does his background stippling under a microscope!

He insists that each dot in the stippling process be precisely placed and exactly like all the rest in the background. This is but one reason why his work is so distinctive and easily recognized.

If an engraving pattern calls for inlay work, either line inlay or animal scenes, the inlay metal to be used, usually gold or silver, must first be permanently attached to the steel of the firearm. This is normally accomplished by undercutting the pattern in the steel. An outline is made of the inlay and the steel under the inlay is removed. The edges of the pattern are then undercut, which forms a dovetail in the steel. The precious metal is then hammered into the area where the steel was cut away. The softer inlay metal flows into the undercuts and locks into place. After this task is complete, the inlay can be molded, sculpted, and shaded.

Some engravers will only do one style of engraving, while others will do it all. A few of the best Italian engravers will only execute the *bulino* scenes on a project and will farm out the embellishing scrollwork

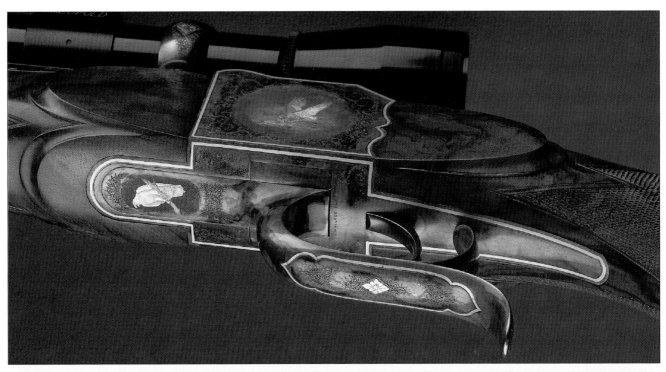

Two views of an absolutely magnificent rifle. Maurice Ottmar built this Hagn action single-shot. It was then sent to Terry Wallace for the exquisite engraving and gold inlay work. Photo by Gary Bolster.

to other engravers. Some engravers are very versatile in their styling, while others are much more limited. It is up to the client to select the desired style of engraving and, once that happens, to find an engraver who will best fulfill this desire.

Only one's checkbook and the calendar limit what is available to a client. A pal of mine recently took delivery of a wonderful Westley Richards best quality double rifle. Although he loves English doubles, he is not particularly enamored with its typical factory engraving. He had the rifle delivered unadorned and sent it to a favored American engraver, Ken Warren, to execute the embellishment. Perhaps 99 percent of all double rifle aficionados would be enthralled with a new Westley Richards double, direct from the factory. My friend is the exception, but he got what he wanted.

We often look back on the good old days with fondness and nostalgia. A frequently heard subject of discussion when a group of gun nuts get together, focuses on the theme that "they just don't make things like they used to." Depending on the particular item under discussion, there is often merit to the argument. Even so, when custom guns or engraving is the subject of the discussion, this scribe has no desire to return to yesteryear. I believe that the highest quality custom firearms as well as the most artistic and exquisite engraving in our history, are being turned out today.

Even better, judging from the talents of newcomers in the business today and the quality of their work, the best is yet to come.

Although engraving is the primary art form used to embellish firearms of all types, there are others. One that is seldom seen in the US but often encountered in Europe is stock carving. Both the Germans and the Austrians are masters at this art form. I have seen everything from a small amount of delicate scrollwork carved into a stock to fighting stags and charging wild boar boldly leaping from the wood. I have seen sculpted ivory and in one case, silver inlaid into the stock for added emphasis. Such work, while generally beautifully executed, is not for me, though. I can certainly appreciate the talent and artistry required to execute such a job, but not on my guns. My custom rifle pal with the glitz and glitter taste would probably kill to have such work embellishing his rifles.

One of the nicest jobs I have seen recently was on a rifle owned and engraved by Marty Rabeno. Rabeno started with a restored Winchester Model 73 chambered for the .22 rimfire and executed a magnificent *bulino* engraving job on the rifle. He then sent it to Joe Rundell for a superbly executed carving job on the stock. Rundell carved delicate scrollwork into the stock and on this particular piece, it really fits with the flow of the overall rifle.

Another embellishment used often by the Germans and Austrians is fish scale checkering. Actually, it isn't checkering at all but a form of carving. I think that it looks pretty spiffy on handgun grips, but a bit much on a fine rifle or shotgun. I had one rifle stocked in Germany that, in a weak moment, I allowed my engraver pal to do a fish scale job on. The work was beautifully executed, but just didn't jive with my taste. I found someone who loved it and traded him the rifle.

Contrasting wood inlays in a stock, generally popularized in this country by Roy Weatherby, is another form of decoration that I can do without. Designed with imagination and executed with skill and precision, inlays can be attractive. I once owned a custom rifle that featured inlays in the stock. At the time, I liked them very much. I have also owned a couple factory Weatherby rifles over the years that had inlays in the stock. These days, though, none of my guns are so decorated. I look upon stock inlays like I do convertible top cars and home swimming pools. Everyone has to have one sometime in their life. One such experience, though, is usually enough.

One form of embellishment I do like, however, is scrimshaw designs on ivory handgun or knife grips. I have an engraved Smith & Wesson Model 39 handgun that my German engraver friend Erich Boessler did a job on. Included in the job was a pair of ivory grips that Boessler expertly crafted and then scrimshawed. He also did a matching engraving/ scrimshaw job on a custom Bowie-type knife that Gil Hibben made for me. I think the set is pretty spiffy and I like it a lot. I have it out in the shop of Jim Hasson at the moment. Hasson is fashioning one of his superb custom wooden cases to house the set. Boessler finished the set for me more than twenty years ago, so it is high time I provided an adequate setting for it. I only recently met Hasson and learned of the magnificent work he is doing in wood. Perhaps it was fate that kept me from doing something with the set earlier.

As it is with everything else in custom guns, the selection of embellishment styles and forms are deeply personal decisions and reflect the taste or lack thereof of the owner.

Chapter 9

Custom Engravers

ngraving was not a particular talent that was evident among the early Americans. While factory-engraved Colt and Winchester firearms are highly prized and very expensive collectors' items these days, the factory engravers' names are not typical American names. Just about every gun nut has heard of the likes of L.D. Nimschke, the prolific Ulrich family, Cuno Helfricht, and Gustave Young (read Jung). These engravers were all linked to factory-engraved Colt and Winchester guns. Later, such names as Arnold Griebel, R.J. Kornbrath, Max Bruehl, and Josef Fugger were prominent to engraving aficionados. Of course, with such family names, all were of German origin.

For some reason, Germany has produced many fine engravers for eons and still does today. Whether they possess a special Teutonic engraving gene in their makeup or not, I can't say. What I can say is that many superb engravers carry Germanic family names. From the nineteenth century and perhaps before, well into the twentieth century, most well-known engravers in this country were of Germanic origin.

One of the first non-Germanic engravers I became aware of was E.C. (Jack) Prudhomme. A Louisiana native, Prudhomme began his engraving career in the 1940s. Besides executing wonderful engraving, Prudhomme also wrote about it. His book, *The Gun Engraving Review*, was well received and about the only book on the subject at the time. The book has been out of print for many years now and when a copy can be found, collectors go after it eagerly.

Another non-Germanic engraver who became well-known was A.A. White. The Massachusetts native started his career even earlier than did Prudhomme. White devoted much of his work to Colt revolvers, so much so that he was often thought to be a Colt employee. He wasn't and spent most of his career as an independent craftsman. During the '60s and early '70s, he was the chief engraver for A.A.

White Engravers, Inc., and worked for himself during all but that period.

Two engravers who plied their trade for many years were often thought to be brothers. As best I can figure out, though, they were not related. Floyd Warren was a native Buckeye, born in Kinsman, Ohio, and the other, John Warren, was a New Englander from Massachusetts. I became acquainted with the work of both men from reading the pages of *Gun Digest*. It was a rare issue of the *Digest* that didn't showcase the artistry of one Warren or the other and often, both had examples of their work in the book.

Another engraver, James B. Meek, in addition to engraving guns and doing oil paintings, wrote a how-to book called *The Art of Engraving*. He did so because there was no such manual in print that he could find. I believe his book is still in print and has been available for years from the publisher, Brownells. Most of the Brownells catalogs from several years ago were illustrated with Meek's paintings.

These and many other engravers provided the transition from almost totally Germanic engravers to guys with names like Churchill, McKenzie, Smith, Wallace, Evans, Rabeno, Shostle, Swartley, Welch, and Viramontez. There are still a fair number of engravers with Germanic names doing great work in this country, along with several of Italian origin.

The rest of this chapter consists of short bios of some current engravers busy at their benches around the country, along with a photo of each engraver's work. The list is by no means exhaustive nor could it be in a book of this size. It is, I think, fairly representative of the quality of engraving available to the aficionado who appreciates fine engraving.

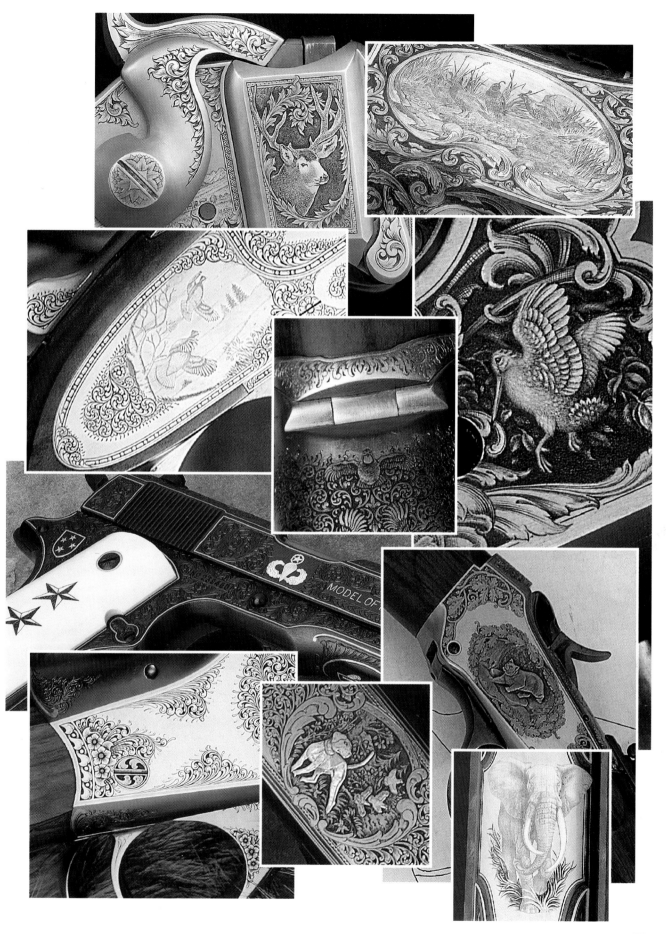

John Barraclough

John Barraclough is a most interesting fellow. Born and raised in England, he started his career as a steeplechase jockey. His pay, as he related to me, was room and board in a small English town. As a jockey, he was often banged up with an odd injury and while recuperating, there was little to do in the burg where he lived. There was a gunmaker in the town, though. Barraclough, during those periods of convalescence, hung out at the old gunmaker's shop. He would give the old boy a hand in performing tasks that he could do. The fellow wasn't an engraver, but he did do small engraving jobs as a part of the rest of his work. He considered the engraving as a component part of the total job. That was Barraclough's introduction to the art of engraving.

Barraclough moved to the United States and had a commercial interior design business for many years. He also bought a piece of land in California and developed it into an avocado farm. Lassen Community College in Susanville, in association with the NRA, announced that it was offering the NRA summer school in engraving, to be taught by Neil Hartliep. Barraclough attended the program and began his engraving career shortly thereafter. These days, he teaches engraving programs at both Lassen and Trinidad State Junior College. He estimates that about 600 students have taken his classes in engraving. From 1948 when he first dabbled in engraving, until about 1980 when he got serious with his engraving career, he did many things. Since getting serious, though, he has restricted his activities to engraving and avocado farming. He executes all styles of engraving, but most enjoys the American style. He also relishes working on period American pieces such as early Winchesters and Colt revolvers.

This 20ga. Winchester Model 12 was engraved and gold inlaid by John Barraclough. The gun is blued with selective French gray on the sides of the receiver. Multi-color gold is used for the inlay work. Photo by Walter Rickell.

Jim Blair

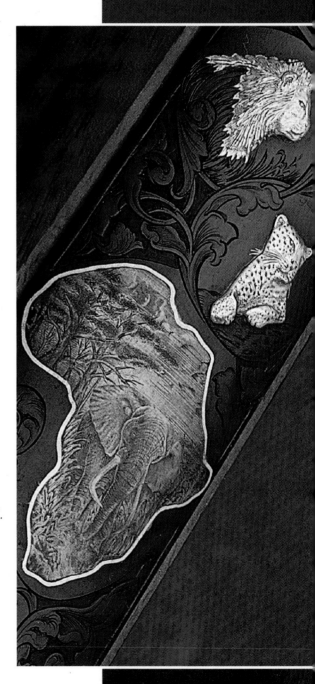

Jim Blair was born in Lander, Wyoming, and has lived in that state for his entire life. During the period before he turned to engraving as a livelihood, he worked on ranches, for the Forest Service, as an auto body repairman, a painter, and as a teacher and welder at a coal mine. He began his training for engraving in 1980. He attended training at the NRA school in Trinidad, Colorado, with classes taught by Neil Hartliep, John Barrenclough, Sam Welch, and Robert Swartley. He taught himself the rest.

He prefers to work with light, delicate scrollwork, with lots of definition. He also prefers game scenes cut in a bulino style. He does 90 percent of his work with hammer and graver and the remainder with a burin. He also does some knives and dies for limited edition prints.

A custom Model 70 Winchester in .375 H&H caliber served as the canvas for Wyoming engraver Jim Blair. Custom maker Roger Green did both the metal work and the stock for the rifle. Photo by Alan Richmond.

Erich Boessler

rich Boessler was the first engraver I got to know personally and has been a close friend of mine for almost thirty years now. In fact, it was largely due to him that I got into the writing business. To condense an otherwise very long story, I was very familiar with his work long before I ever met him. He had done much of the engraving for a large US operation for many years, and I had seen his work publicized in most of the American gun magazines. His work, though, was always credited to the company that had engaged him. While understandable, I felt it was somewhat unfair that his name was totally unknown in this country. I wrote a story about him and his work, which was published as my very first story to see print.

Born in the former East Germany, Boessler escaped over the Iron Curtain in the dead of night. He crossed the border and settled in the first town he came to. As it turned out, the Heym factory had done the same thing and settled in the same town. He worked for Heym as one of its factory engravers for awhile and then hung out his shingle in private practice. He has taught many of today's finest German engravers and although mostly retired now, he still accepts a few jobs each year. As he told me, he does only those jobs he wants to do these days.

Note: Boessler passed away in May 1997 at age 69.

....

German Master Engraver Erich Boessler did all the engraving on this Heym sidelock double rifle. Not only is Boessler a wounderful engraver, but he is also an outstanding teacher. Numerous Master Engravers in the old country received their training in the Boessler shop. Photo courtesy F.W. Heym.

Winston Churchill

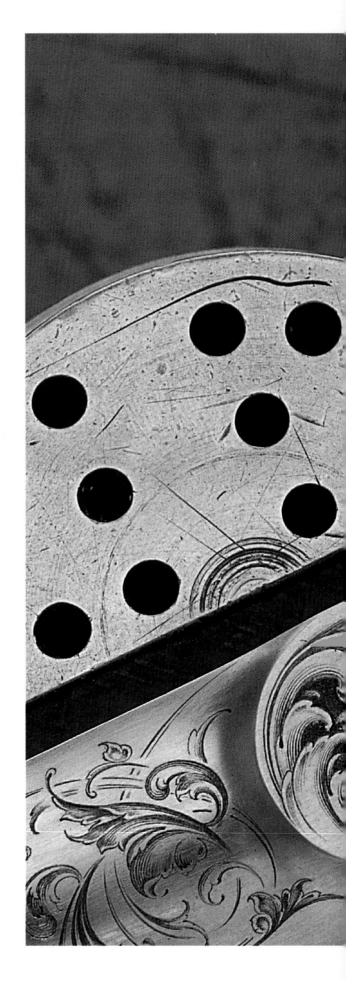

A native New Englander, Winston Churchill has been considered by most as one of the very best engravers in the world for many years now. He began his career with firearms by making a stock for a shotgun at the ripe old age of thirteen. After school and a tour of duty with the US Navy, he went to work for Griffin & Howe in New York. There he studied under Master Engraver Josef Fugger. Although he had taught himself the basics of engraving before moving to New York, he improved and expanded his skills under the watchful eye of Fugger. He also did stockwork in addition to engraving while at Griffin & Howe.

After a few years at the NY firm, he returned to his native Vermont and set up shop as an independent engraver. He has been at it since. Churchill does only top quality work and his trademark is very fine detailed work. He has engraved many of the finest firearms ever built. Recently, he has expanded his output to include bronze sculptures.

A spectacular engraving job in progress in Winston Churchill's shop. The gun, by the way, is a 28 bore Parker. Photo courtesy of Winston Churchill.

Mike Dubber

M̃ike Dubber has been engraving firearms since 1969. He received Bachelor and Masters Degrees in Fine Arts from Indiana State University and his career areas have included teaching fine arts, six years in jewelry manufacturing and sales, advertising, and public relations. He gained his knowledge of firearms engraving through practical experience and by working with master gunsmiths.

Dubber's favored subjects are bolt action and single-shot rifles. He works in English, German, and American scrolls and enjoys doing sculptured gold inlaid game scenes. As a personal aside, his work, while always very good, has really reached a new plateau of excellence in the past couple years.

Desert Storm hero General H. Norman Schwarzkopf was the recipient of this Government Model Colt .45. The pistol was commissioned specifically for presentation to the General. Mike Dubber did all the engraving on the gun and personally presented it to General Schwarzkopf. Photo by Mike Borchert.

Bob Evans

Bob Evans is a full-time engraver with more than twenty years experience. He is also the current historian of the Firearms Engravers Guild of America. Evans, who grew up in Oklahoma, developed a strong interest in firearms during his childhood. He taught high school history and he refined his skills during his off time. He enjoyed building muzzle-loading rifles and took up engraving when he had problems finding someone to engrave his creations. Later, he gave up building rifles to concentrate on his engraving.

He works with all styles of engraving, but prefers to execute small Germanic scrollwork, blackleaf, high quality gold work, or bulino scenes. He executes much of his work under a microscope.

The engraving talents of Bob Evans are readily apparent in this photo. Pete Mazur did all the metalwork on the L.C. Smith shotgun and Steve Billeb crafted the stock. Photo by Mustafa Bilal.

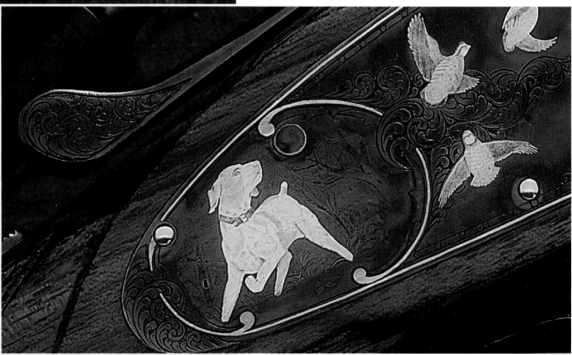

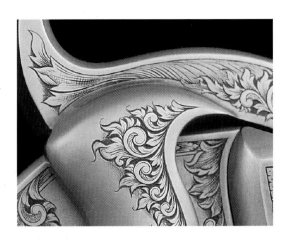

William Gamradt

Bill Gamradt is a professional engraver and artist, who lives in Missoula, Montana. He spends a good deal of time—as much as being absent from the bench and/or canvas will permit—out in the boonies of his home state. He believes that the photographs and sketches of the area's big game and landscapes that he collects from these field trips are essential to better his work. He uses the collected pictures in both his engraving and his artwork.

Besides engraving, Gamradt owns and operates an art gallery in Missoula where he sells his original oil paintings and etchings of wildlife and landscapes. His lifelong career as an artist provided a background that, coupled with his interests in hunting and firearms, led him smoothly into firearms engraving about ten years ago.

Montana engraver and artist Bill Gamradt likes to work on period pieces. This Shiloh Sharps recreation of a Sharps Long Range Express rifle is a perfect recipient of Gamradt's work. Photo by the engraver.

$\mathcal{E}$ric $\mathcal{G}$old

$\mathcal{E}$ric Gold has been a full-time engraver since 1975. Although largely self taught, Gold is quick to credit the advice and assistance of many professional engravers early in his career. He spent a number of years restoring the engraving on fine shotguns. He specializes in small English rose and scroll, leaf and vine, American scroll and animal scenes in semi-relief, and bulino.

The combined talents of gunmaker Steven Dodd Hughes and engraver Eric Gold produced this exquisite Hughes-Fox 20 bore shotgun. Gold's engraving as well as his pre-engraving drawings are shown in this Steven Dodd Hughes photo

Barry Lee Hands

Barry Lee Hands began engraving professionally in 1979 at the age of nineteen. He is largely self-taught, but credits Ethan Jacczak and Dan Goodwin with teaching him the basics of tool sharpening and design. He creates beautiful pieces in many different styles including arabesque, English, Victorian, and American scroll. His work is often highlighted with 24k gold figures and borders. Hands lives and works in the Big Sky country of Montana, on the shore of Flathead Lake.

Ted Blackburn was the metalsmith and Gary Goudy the stockmaker on this lovely 7x57 Mauser rifle. Barry Lee Hands engraved the rifle in a traditional English scroll pattern. Photo by Weyer.

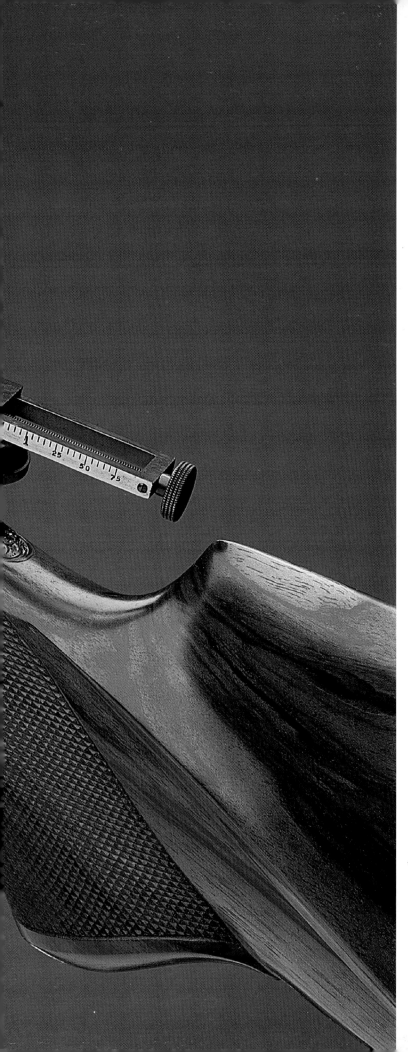

Frank Hendricks

first became aware of Frank Hendricks' work in an article written by the late Elmer Keith. Keith wrote about a new rifle that had been built for him by Champlin Arms—at the time known as Champlin & Haskins, I believe. Keith had done some design work for the company and it built him the Keith Grade rifle, presumably as a reward for his work. It was beautifully engraved and gold inlaid by Hendricks.

Hendricks began his engraving career while on active duty with the US Air Force in Germany. He studied under German Master Engraver Kurt Rechnagel to refine and polish his already considerable skills. He began engraving professionally in 1961. Hendricks, a native Texan, has a shop in San Antonio.

Frank Hendricks engraved the 1997 American Custom Gunmakers Guild raffle project. One of two guns in the project, the metalwork was done by Bob Snapp and the stock by Steven Dodd Hughes. Photo by Mustafa Bilal.

Ralph Ingle

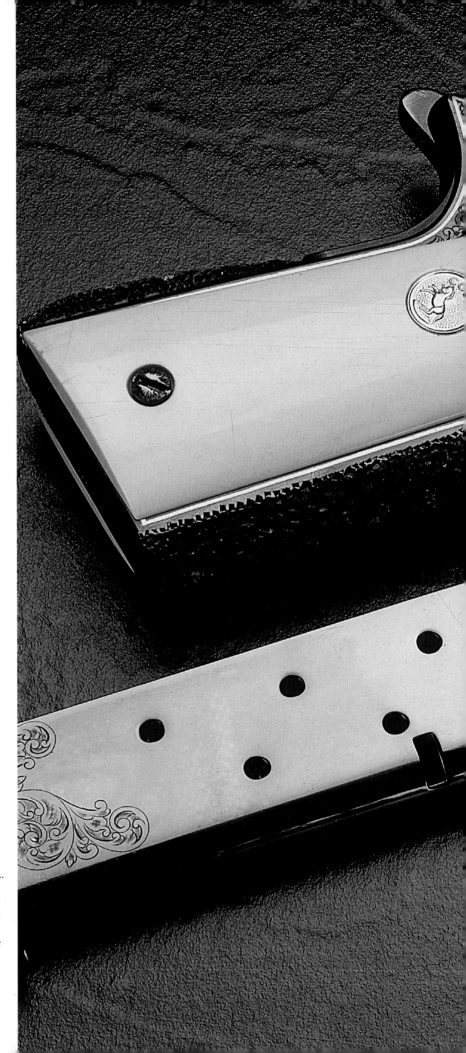

Ralph Ingle was born in Tennessee, but now lives and works in Georgia. He began his engraving career in the early 1960s engraving Coca-Cola molds, with an apprenticeship under the watchful and critical eye of Master Engraver Roy Westbrooks. As he refined his skills, he began doing minor engraving jobs for his coworkers. When he felt capable, he established his shop and began accepting commissions for engraving jobs. He now engraves firearms and knives and has clients all over the world. He prefers to execute English and German floral scroll and does all his work with the traditional hammer and chisel method.

A Government Model Colt .45 auto from the shop of Ralph Ingle. The engraving is Germanic scroll and is cut using the traditional hammer and chisel. Photo courtesy of Ralph Ingle.

$\mathcal{L}$ynton $\mathcal{M}c\mathcal{K}$enzie

$\mathcal{A}$ legend among American engravers, Lynton McKenzie was born in Australia. At a very early age, he took up shooting and working on muzzle-loading arms, which is something he still enjoys. He taught himself to engrave using the traditional hammer, chisel, and burin. When he had progressed about as far as he could go by himself, he left Australia. There were no other engravers in Australia whom he could learn from. He settled in London where he engraved for such prestigious firms as Holland & Holland, Rigby, Westley Richards, Purdey, and most of the other London gunmakers. At Purdey, for whom most of his work was done, he worked with Ken Hunt, England's best known engraver.

In about 1970, McKenzie moved to the United States, and settled first in New Orleans. There he worked with the New Orleans Arms Co., and turned out a remarkable number of museum quality pieces. Many of these pieces were publicized in national magazines. He remained in New Orleans until 1978 and then relocated to Colorado for a couple years. There he worked closely with master gunmaker Richard Hodgson. In 1980, McKenzie again relocated, this time to Tucson, Arizona, where he still resides. Recently, McKenzie has been quite ill and, as I understand it, is not accepting any new clients at the present time. Hopefully, that will not last long.

The magnificent work of Lynton McKenzie on a David Miller Co. custom rifle. Lynton is one of America's best and best known engravers. Photo by Ron Dehn.

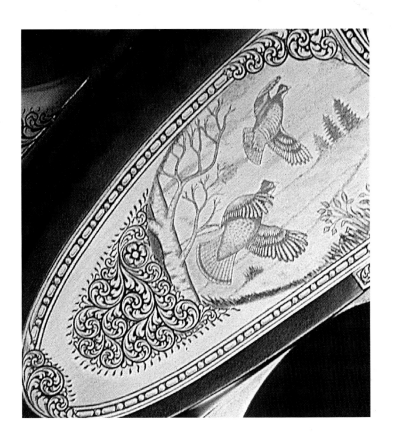

Rex Pedersen

ex Pedersen is a third generation gunsmith who began his engraving career in 1978. Growing up in the gun business in Michigan, he performed many different gunsmithing operations before specializing in engraving. He had been a board member of the Firearms Engravers Guild of America for many years and now serves as the secretary of that organization. He has been commissioned to do engravings for Ducks Unlimited in several states. Anhauser Busch and Ducks Unlimited in Michigan and Illinois have commissioned a shotgun each year, the sale of which has raised over $250,000 to date for their conservation programs. He has also accomplished presentation engraving work for the Amway Corporation.

Rex Pedersen engraved this lovely Browning Superposed 28 bore shotgun, that is fit with sideplates. The addition of sideplates to the boxlock gun provides the engraver with much more space to execute more lavish engraving patterns. Photo by Russ Miller.

Marty Rabeno

Marty Rabeno was born and raised in New York City. His background in the arts has served him well in his career as an engraver. He received a thorough education in the arts, from high school through graduate school. He also teaches high school art. He began engraving firearms in 1976, on muzzle-loading guns he had made. He approaches engraving firearms as an extension of his fine arts training in that each piece he does is somewhat unique, while he retains the qualities of good design and execution. He specializes in American and Victorian scroll, heavily shaded for the 3-D effect. He also likes flush line inlays, game scenes in gold or bulino, and monograms. As a personal aside, while all his work is exquisite, I believe that his very best work is his bulino engraving.

Rabeno is a founding member of the Firearms Engravers Guild of America (FEGA) and served as vice president of FEGA for eleven years. He has been the president of the guild since January 1996.

....

New York engraver Mary Rabeno chose his personal Winchester Model 73 .22 rimfire rifle to receive this magnificent pattern. A combination of original Winchester style scrollwork, combined with Rabeno's bulino, or banknote, scenes, the job is wonderful. Photo by Alan Richmond.

Roger Sampson

Roger Sampson's study of engraving began in 1982 at the Pine Technical Institute under the instruction of Austrian trained engraver Emma Achleithner. His training has been amplified over the years thanks to the guild engravers that have served as instructors for the NRA summer school programs. He has now held positions as an engraving instructor at the Pine Technical College for both the NRA summer schools program and an elective program in engraving offered by the college.

He has been an active member of FEGA since 1984 and was awarded professional member status in 1989. He has served as a member of the FEGA board of directors. In addition to his work on firearms and hand crafted knives, he is well-known for his work as an engraver of miniature firearms.

Roger Sampson executed the engraving on this custom Model 21 Winchester. Although this Model 21 is a full-size gun, Sampson specializes in engraving miniature firearms. Photo by Alan Richmond.

ℬ𝓇𝓊𝒸𝑒 𝒮𝒽𝒶𝓌

𝒜 graduate mechanical engineer, Bruce Shaw received his art training at Cal State University in Los Angeles. He started engraving in 1978 and graduated to full-time status in 1984. He specializes in pistols with American scroll and deeply carved game animals. He also does a number of Native American designs with deeply carved figures.

This unusual engraving job is the work of Bruce Shaw. Executing a Native American design on an all-American firearm like the Thompson/Center Contender is appropriate. Photo courtesy of Bruce Shaw.

Ben Shostle

en Shostle, a fellow Kentuckian, has lived in Indiana for many years. A self-taught engraver, he has been at the bench for a long time. In addition to his engraving talents, he is also a skilled gunsmith and stockmaker. In fact, he got into engraving to broaden his skills as a 'smith and stockmaker. The tail ended up wagging the dog! A former president of the FEGA, Shostle is not only a fine engraver, but a true gentleman as well.

This heavily engraved and ivory stocked Luger is the work of former Firearms Engravers Guild of America President, Ben Shostle. Photo courtesy of the Firearms Engravers Guild of America.

Ron Smith

$\mathcal{R}$on Smith was, to me at least, a well-kept secret. While I try to keep current on all custom gun work going on around the country, I was totally unaware of his magnificent engraving until the 1995 guild exhibition. At that function, I served as a judge for the Firearms Marketing Group Award of Excellence competition. The winner of that competition was an exquisite single-shot rifle built by Maurice Ottmar and engraved by one Ron Smith. The rifle and the engraving were, in a word, magnificent. A Texan, Smith excels at all phases of the engraver's art. He can do it all and do it extraordinarily well. His inlaid game scenes are remarkably exquisite.

This Holland & Holland double rifle is the recipient of the masterful engraving of Texan Ron Smith. It just don't get any better than this. Photo courtesy of the Firearms Engravers Guild of America.

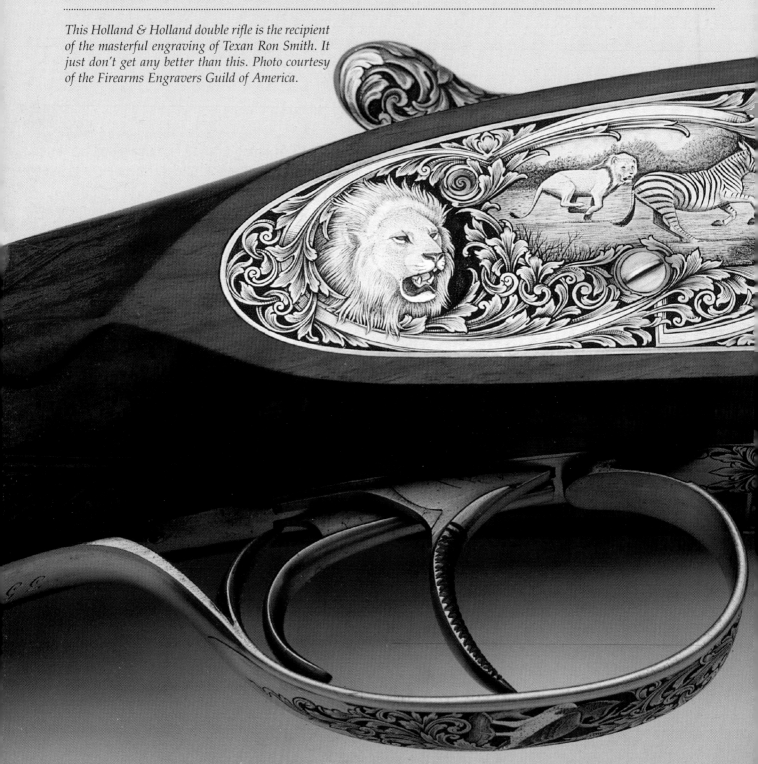

Robert Swartley

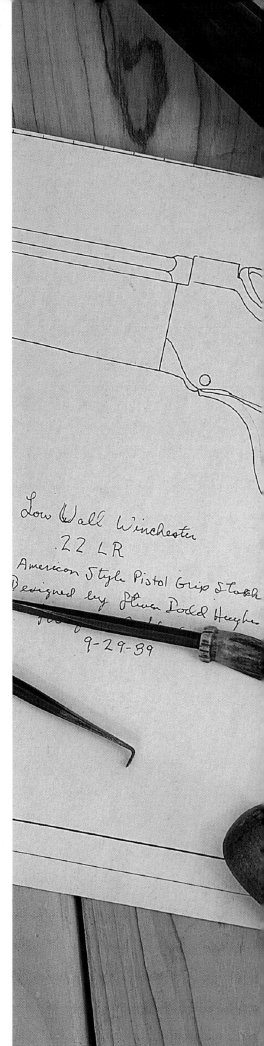

obert Swartley has been involved with firearms and engraving for more than thirty years. He started by graduating from gunsmithing school at the Colorado School of Trades. Shortly after graduating, he served for two years in the US Army where he was a member of the Army rifle team. After military service, he was employed by Griffin & Howe in New York City. There, like his fellow engraver Winston Churchill, he worked with Master Engraver Josef Fugger. After two years with Griffin & Howe, he opened his own business as an independent engraver.

Swartley, like most all accomplished engravers, executes his work in a very distinctive style. His work can be recognized as far away as it can be seen by knowledgeable enthusiasts.

Californian Bob Swartley was chosen to engrave this Steven Dodd Hughes Winchester Low Wall .22 rimfire rifle. Swartley's engraving is very distinctive in style and can be immediately recognized by knowledgeable viewers. Photo by Steven Dodd Hughes.

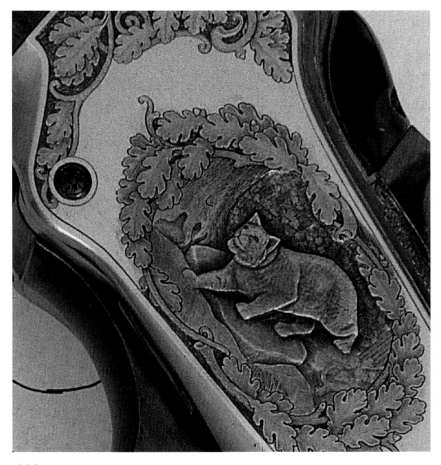

Notes: ① Very low cheekpiece
          like Ballard Schuetzen.
        ② Pistol Grip early Winchester profile.
        ③ Deep groove at rear of grip. forms
        ④ Suggested sights; Tang PREP rear. blade o
        ⑤ although this style has a larger buttstock it will be a

Terry Theis

Terry Theis is another engraver I was not familiar with prior to starting this book. Theis called me one day to inquire about sending some photos of his work for inclusion in the book. In our conversation, as he was giving me some of his background, he told me that he had studied in the shop of one of Germany's finest engravers. As I knew many of the engravers there, I asked him which one he had studied under. My jaw dropped to the floor when he answered that he had worked under my old friend Erich Boessler. That was an exceptionally long phone call because he brought me up to date on my friend.

Theis began engraving in 1983 and now works at his chosen craft full time. His Germanic training is reflected in his work, although he executes engravings in all the major styles.

A pair of Winchester Model 23 .410ga shotguns as engraved by Terry Theis: Theis received his training in Germany and the influence of the Germanic school of engraving on him is clearly evident in this photo. Photo by Marc Bennett.

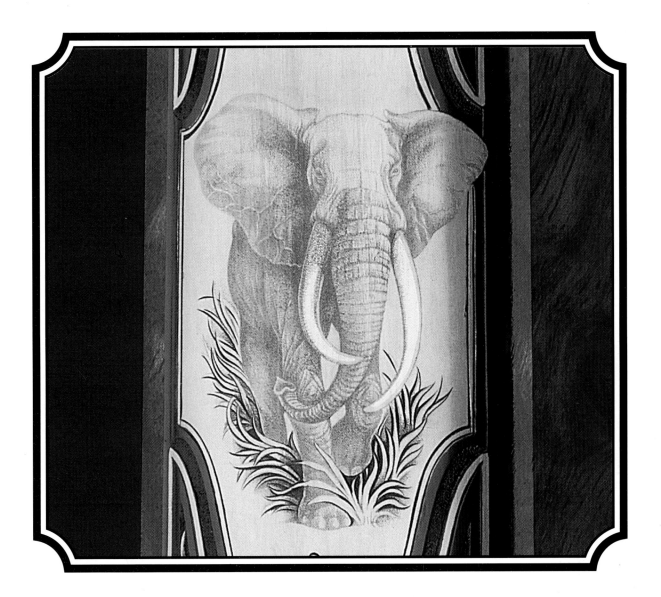

𝓛𝒾𝓈𝒶 𝒯𝑜𝓂𝓁𝒾𝓃

𝓛isa Tomlin is an exception in the male-dominated field of engraving. A southern belle from Virginia, I first learned of her work from a good friend of mine. Somehow, he had found out about her and commissioned her to do some work for him. He was so pleased with it that he sent me some photos. I was also duly impressed. Her engraving is delicate and her game scene inlays are wonderfully done. She was selected to engrave the Elephant Rifle, the final rifle in the Safari Club International series of five guns commemorating the world's dangerous game animals. The rifle, built by John Bolliger's Mountain Riflery and engraved by Tomlin, sold at auction for $165,000.

....

Lisa Tomlin engraved the Elephant Rifle, the final rifle in the Safari Club International series of five rifles commemorating dangerous game animals of the world. John Bolliger built the rifle. Photo by Mustafa Bilal.

Terry Wallace

A self-taught engraver, Terry Wallace began engraving professionally in 1964. His main source of information was Prudhomme's book, Gun Engraving Review. He also studied and was influenced by the work of L.D. Nimschke and Rudolph Kornbrath. He was fortunate to meet and exchange ideas with Robert Swartley and feels that his style and influences have helped in establishing his manner of engraving. He works full time at his art and works in all the major styles of engraving. Wallace is an avid outdoorsman and enjoys both hunting and fishing. He is a very versatile engraver and all his work is superb.

An exquisite Browning Superposed shotgun engraved by Terry Wallace. Photo by Gary Bolster.

Frank R. Wells — Riflemaker
Kenneth W Warren — Engraver

Ken Warren

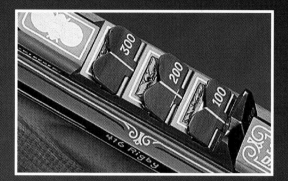

A gun collector and competitive shooter for years, Ken Warren decided in 1969 to learn how to engrave as a hobby. Unfortunately, he didn't have access to a school or another engraver, so he taught himself by trial and error. After several months of using the push graver, chase hammer, and chisel, he achieved some modest success. After years of studying other engravers' work and visiting such museums as Smithsonian and the Winchester museum, he developed the ability to execute the different types of cuts required to create the various styles of scrollwork.

In 1979, Warren decided to make better use of his engraving abilities. He quit his bread and butter job and moved, with his wife and two children, to Arizona. There, he began establishing his reputation as an engraver and laying the groundwork to open his engraving business. He started engraving full time in 1983. Since then he has engraved several guns for SCI and recently completed a set of double rifles for Westley Richards. This latter set was engraved in sculpted deep relief, one of his specialties.

Ken Warren engraved this exquisite rifle for Safari Club International to be sold at auction to raise funds to support that organization's conservation efforts around the world. The rifle was built by Frank Wells. Photo by Ron Dehn.

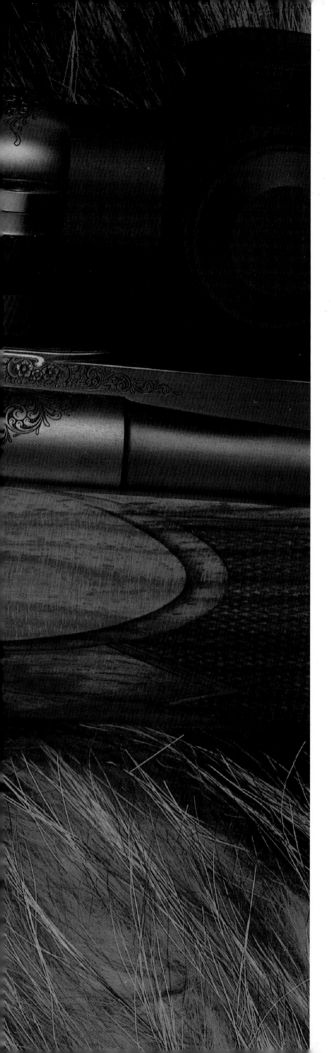

Sam Welch

Sam Welch was born and raised in Arkansas. After he finished college with a degree in mathematics and a minor in physics, he entered the US Air Force. In 1966, while stationed at Turner Air Force Base in Georgia, he met Ray Viramontez. Viramontez was also in the Air Force but spent his spare time engraving. Welch was most impressed with his work. Viramontez taught him the basics of engraving and they worked together until both men were transferred to different bases. Welch continued to study engraving until 1968 when he left the Air Force. He picked up his engraving again in 1974 when he was living in Alaska, and started his engraving business in 1978.

Welch now lives in Utah and engraves full time. He has served on the board of directors of the FEGA, and served as both vice president and president of the organization. He specializes in German scroll and blackleaf, sculptured oak leaves and inlays. He also does bulino engraving. He works on firearms and knives and also does scrimshaw and jewelry work.

This Don Klein High Wall custom rifle was engraved by Sam Welch. The lovely combination of floral decoration and scrollwork is typical of work coming from the Welch shop. Photo courtesy of Sam Welch.

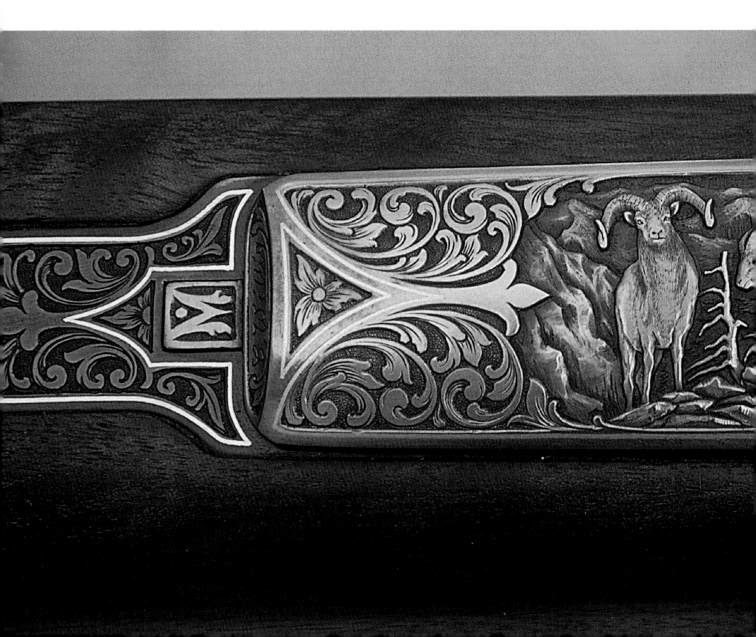

Claus Willig

aster Engraver Claus Willig is one of Germany's finest engravers and one of the best known here in the US. The son of a master engraver, Willig grew up engraving in his father's shop. He was represented in America by Jaeger's for many years and is still represented by Dietrich Apel of New England Custom Guns. Apel is the nephew of the late Paul Jaeger and the former owner of Jaeger's. Willig engraved the Lion Rifle, Jaeger's contribution to the Safari Club International "Guns of the Big Five" series a few years ago. The Lion Rifle sold at auction for $140,000.

A very versatile engraver, Willig can do everything from tiny English scrollwork to bulino scenes to deeply carved Germanic engraving. More importantly, he executes each style of engraving flawlessly. He is a good friend of mine and I have followed his career for many years. From the time I first met him more than twenty years ago, his work has been outstanding. I believe that he is doing the best work of his long career right now. He just gets better and better.

German master engraver Claus Willig did the engraving on this floorplate. The son of a master engraver, Claus has worked for American customers for years. Photo by the engraver.

Chapter 10

The Specialists

*I*n a field as wide as the custom gun trade is, a few craftsmen and women have specialized in one aspect or the other of the trade. Most of them are certainly capable of expertly executing many other facets involved in crafting the custom gun. Some, though, have become so well-known, so expert, and so busy trying to keep up with the work, that they have, by design or by customer demand, concentrated on one particular task. To distinguish these specialists and their contributions to the general betterment of the custom gun of today, I have included a listing of some of them, along with a short bio, and a photo example of each specialist's work. There are many others plying their trade and this short list is not intended to slight those not mentioned. Space limitations and, in some cases, simply not having a photo of their work, has kept the list rather short.

Ted Blackburn

*T*ed Blackburn is an old timer in the custom gun business. He is a superb metalsmith and has turned out many fine custom rifles in addition to his specialty field. He is, I believe, best known for his custom bottom metal, though. Before Blackburn started producing his superb magazine boxes and triggerguard/floorplate combinations and offering them to the trade, custom 'smiths had to modify the existing bottom metal or spend many hours fabricating their own. With Blackburn-produced boxes available, most gave up doing the job themselves and ordered from him. There are very few makers that have not taken advantage of his outstanding work.

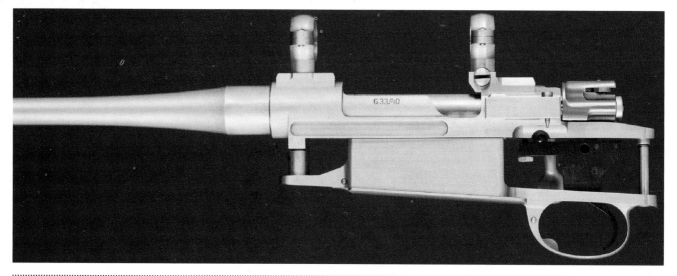

This superb metalsmithing job is not by Ted Blackburn, although he is one of the best metalsmiths around. Rather, it is by Bruce Russell. In this particular job, it is the trigger that is from the Blackburn shop. Blackburn is best known for his custom bottom metal, but he can do it all. Photo by Steven Dodd Hughes.

Kathy Forster

A major task that many stockmakers would just as soon leave to someone else is checkering. Top quality checkering is tedious and time consuming to execute, not to mention an easy way to go stark raving nuts! Most quality stockmakers can do exquisite checkering, but not many that I know enjoy doing it. In addition, not every stockmaker can do precise checkering with the same quality as the rest of their stocks. I have seen several stocks that were absolutely superbly crafted in every aspect except the checkering job. In those cases, the checkering, while good, was not of the same quality as the rest of the work.

Fortunately, there are a few craftspersons around who specialize in nothing but checkering. Oregonian Kathy Forster is one of this small group. Forster learned checkering while employed by Kimber. When the company experienced financial difficulty and was forced to close, Forster went on her own and now does checkering for other craftsmen and women as well as private clients. Her work is clean, precise, and reasonably priced. Many, if not most of her client base, are professional stockmakers. That is high tribute to her skills.

Checkering is an arduous chore that many stockmakers do not particularly enjoy doing. Fortunately, there are specialists out there that do nothing but. Kathy Forster is one such specialist. She does beautiful work and apparently enjoys doing it.

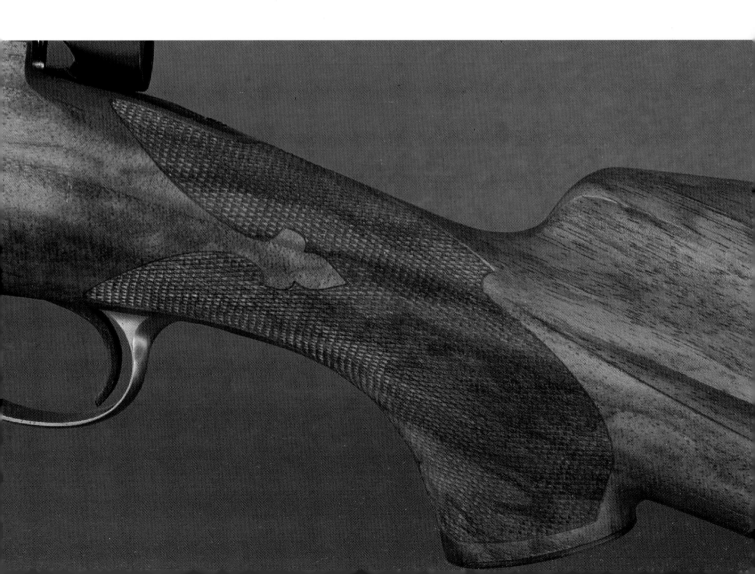

Jim Hasson

*J*im Hasson is a newcomer to the business. His specialty is crafting magnificent hardwood display cases for presentation or museum quality firearms. I first met Hasson, an Arizonan, at a gun show in Phoenix although I had corresponded with him earlier. He brought along a couple of his creations to show me the quality work that he was doing. To say that I was duly impressed is an understatement. The two cases I saw were both done for himself and featured the finest contrasting wood inlay work that I have ever seen. He replicated the Smith & Wesson logo on one case and the Colt logo on the other and inlayed each with contrasting exotic and domestic hardwoods. He also, with the help of his wife, fabricated silver hinges, hasps, and clasps. The only problem that I could see with his work was the potential difficulty of finding enough clients willing to pay for the hundreds of hours of precise handwork required.

I convinced Hasson to craft a line of cases that, while top quality work in every respect, did not have the very time consuming and expensive inlay work. I was, I think, his first client and I am most pleased with the results. He will execute whatever the client wants, but if the job entails substantial inlay work, the time required—and therefore dollars—is increased substantially. He does outstanding work.

Jim Hasson is a new-comer to the trade, but no one builds a better display case than he does. His work is exceptional as this inlaid Colt display case confirms. Photo by Jerry Jacka.

The British used to have a lock on quality oak-and-leather-type trunk cases. When Marvin Huey came onto the scene, though, he caused them to sit back and take notice. Most exhibition quality firearms crafted in this country are housed and displayed in Huey cases. Photo by Steven Dodd Hughes.

Marvin Huey

arvin Huey's product is seen perhaps more often than any custom maker or engraver's is. That is due to the fact that most of the makers use his product to showcase their work. Huey makes oak-and-leather trunk-type gun cases. He began his work as a hobby and gradually turned it into his full-time profession. His primary occupation for many years was designing stained glass windows. During that period, he built several gun cases for friends. In 1976 he sold his stained glass business and went into building cases in 1977. This year marks the twentieth year he has been at it.

His background in design led Huey to believe that a fine custom firearm deserves a case that will not only protect it, but one that will display it to its best aesthetic advantage. No two custom cases are ever precisely alike just as no two custom guns are identical. Huey feels fortunate to have two wonderful craftspeople working with him. Mike Sweaney, with him for seventeen years, builds the frames, and Ginger Wylie, in the business for two years, does most of the restoration work on older cases. Huey does the bulk of the fitting and he and Sweaney share the leather covering work. These days, it is a rare museum quality firearm that is not housed in a Marvin Huey case.

Dave Talley

ave Talley was a professional fireman for twenty-one years in South Carolina. He also did gunsmithing on the side; he started with general repair work and progressed to building complete guns. In 1976, he retired from the fire department and went into the business basically full time, although he also ran a machine shop producing parts for the textile industry. He and his family moved to Wyoming in 1986 and has operated from there ever since.

Talley is a gifted metalsmith—one of the best. Like Ted Blackburn, however, he is far better known for his accessories than his gunmaking. Although his shop turns out several different items for the gunsmithing trade—gripcaps, sling swivels, barrel band accessories, Mauser floorplates, and several others—his best known item is the scope mount system he makes. Many custom makers use his scope mounts on their creations. Talley, in the business in one fashion or another for thirty-seven years, is contemplating retirement. His son, an able assistant for several years, will take over the business when he retires.

These two Dakota Model 10 single-shot rifles have their scopes mounted in Dave Talley mounts. Talley is a wonderful metalsmith and can do it all, but his scope rings, among other items, have made him a household name in the trade.

135

Doug Turnbull

oug Turnbull worked at Creekside Gun Shop, his family's business, and learned the basics of bone charcoal color case hardening from his father. In the early 1980s, after graduating from college, he began working full time in the shop. His father gave him all the color case work; he refined the process and gained additional knowledge as to how the process works. Turnbull is able to duplicate a variety of case color styles and he is noted for reproducing Parker shotgun colors. Larry Baer, author of The Parker Gun, stated "After observing their work for years, it is my opinion that the color case work done by Terry and Doug Turnbull is the best there is...it is the nearest thing you will find to original Parker colors, and in some cases might have made Parker envious of such beautiful work."

Turnbull has also gained knowledge in how to prevent warpage and has virtually none in his work. Other services include hot, niter, and rust bluing and a complete workshop for metal restoration work.

Color case hardening has, for many years, been a topic of almost mythical proportions. Anyone that could successfully perform this task was viewed as an alchemist or wizard. Doug Turnbull came onto the scene and put a stop to that myth. Turnbull does masterful coloring and his work is second to none—now or in the past. This Winchester was rescued from the trash heap and restored by Ed Webber. Turnbull did the case coloring. Photo by Steven Dodd Hughes.

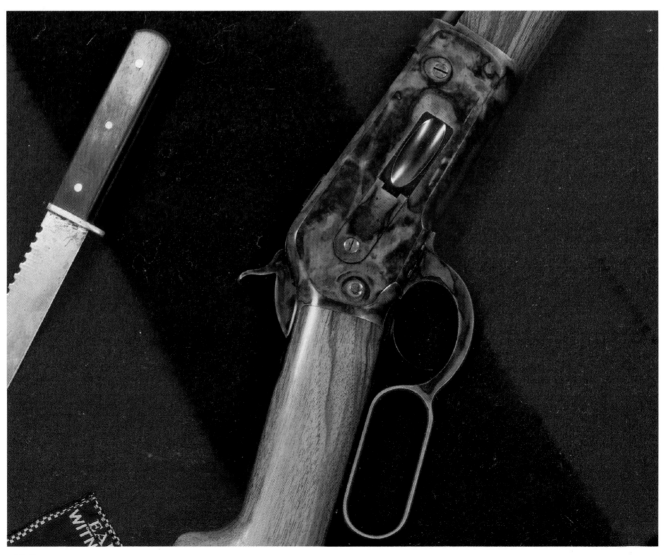

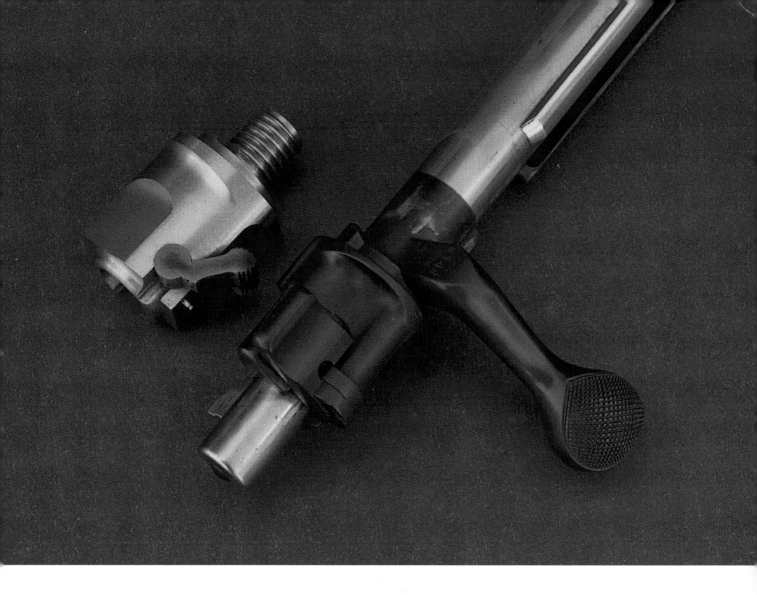

Jim Wisner

J im Wisner was born in Chehalis, Washington, and grew up in his father's business, Wisner's Gun Shop. He began serious work in the shop in 1973 as a stockmaker. He served an apprenticeship as a machinist and has concentrated his skills in recent years as a metalsmith. In 1985 he opened his own business, Precise Metalsmithing Enterprises, Inc., in his home town.

Wisner's business supplies many custom parts to the gunsmithing trade. Some of the items he supplies are Model 70-type safeties for numerous actions, one-piece magazine box/triggerguard units for many different actions, and various sighting arrangements.

Jim Wisner makes many items for the gunmaking trade. One of his items is this replacement cocking piece, including a Winchester Model 70 type side-swing safety.

Chapter 11

The Custom Makers

For a considerable period of our history, the only way to get a new firearm was to go to one of the few gunsmiths in the country and have him build one. All firearms were custom in that era. When the industrial revolution overtook cottage industries, and mass production techniques were developed and refined, factories took over the production role. A customer could have his choice of products rolling off the assembly line. The custom industry didn't completely die, but wasn't exactly robust either.

It remained that way through the end of World War I and for a few years thereafter. Finally, though, with the availability of war surplus firearms at very low prices, demand for custom gun work began to pick up. The surplus Enfields, Springfields, and Mausers were designed for the battlefield, not for hunting. A few independent craftsmen started businesses converting the military armament to instruments for hunting. Most often, this conversion consisted of replacing the military stock and generally cleaning up the metalwork and refinishing it. Sometimes, a new barrel would be fit to the military action, but often the barrel was also retained.

Usually, other than cleaning, polishing, and refinishing, the action was left alone. Sometimes, the military two-stage trigger was either modified or replaced and if one of the new-fangled scopes was the sight of choice of the customer, the safety had to be modified. On occasion, the maker might even modify the magazine box and trigger-

guard to a more pleasing shape.

Between the great wars, bolt action rifles made substantial inroads into the popularity of the lever action for hunting. Remington introduced a sporting rifle based on the Military Model 1917 Enfield in the early 1920s. Winchester followed suit with the predecessor to what would become an industry standard in 1925. Savage had brought out a bolt action sporter in the early 1920s as well.

At about the same time as industry was picking up on the gaining popularity of the bolt action rifle, a few custom houses also opened their doors for business. Hoffman Arms, Griffin & Howe, Niedner Arms, with its best craftsman Tom Shelhamer, R.F. Sedgley, and August Pachmayr (father of Frank), began producing functional and handsome rifles. Some independent craftsmen such as Bob Owen, Alvin Linden, Adolph

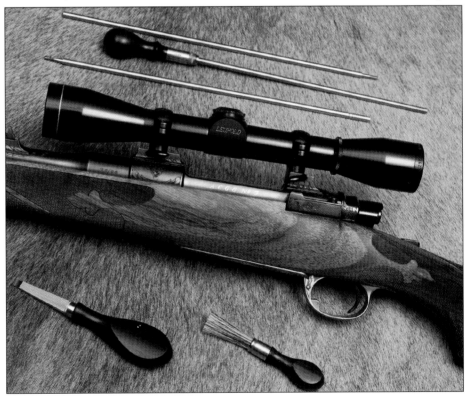

One of the old timers still going strong is Dale Goens. Goens, in his early eighties, still turns out a stock or two each year. This one is a good example of his work. Herman Waldron did the metalwork on the rifle and Mitch Moschetti did the engraving. Photo by Larry Beck.

One of the early makers who got the ball rolling for the trade was R.F. Sedgley. Best known for his 1903 Springfield sporters, Sedgley also did other pieces such as this Winchester High Wall varmint rifle.

One of the true pioneers in the custom gun business was the late Al Linden. Jack O'Connor had Linden craft a few of his custom stocks and often mentioned him in his writings. This Model 70 was built for O'Connor. From the collection of Jim

Minar, and Fred Adolph went about the business of turning out custom stocks that were a vast improvement, both in function and in looks, to factory or surplus stocks.

This fledgling industry came pretty much to a standstill when World War II broke out. After that great war, though, even more surplus rifles were available and the industry, once again, resumed transforming readily available and inexpensive military rifles into more usable hunting guns. As with the earlier effort, most of the conversions were relatively minor and were far more functionally oriented than they were cosmetic. Even so, there were a few craftsmen who apparently decided that life was too short to hunt with an ugly gun. They not only started modifying surplus rifles to function better, but they also began turning them into very attractive guns.

Thanks largely to the outdoor press at the time, some of these small firms and independent craftsmen started attracting attention. Writers Col. Townsend Whelen and Jack O'Connor immediately come to mind. Both howled as if they had been poisoned at the inadequacy of military and factory stocks of the day for hunting. Both praised the efforts of the independent craftsmen in the business of improving the design and craftsmanship of stocks.

Some of the early makers were, to name a few, Monty Kennedy, Lenard Brownell, Leonard Mews, Hal Hartley, Keith Stegall, Gale and Skip Bartlett, Dale Goens, and Al Biesen. Dale Goens is now eighty or so and Al Biesen is in his mid to late seventies. Both these men are still active in the trade. I haven't heard about Keith Stegall in quite some years now, but last I heard, he was still among us. Another icon who is still active is Fred Wells. Wells did it all, except perhaps smelting his own steel, and I'm not even sure that he didn't do that.

Most of these fine artisans were stockmakers, but in this period of custom gun infancy and adolescence, the shooting public paid little attention to metalwork. Over the years, though, that has changed. These days, precise metalwork is every bit as important as the stock, and a very talented group of craftsmen have started specializing in this phase of the custom gun crafting process. The following is a partial listing of custom gunmakers active in the business, along with a short bio of each and a photo example of each custom maker's work. There are many, many more in the trade, but a complete listing is impossible in a book of this length. No slight is intended to those artisans not included in the list, nor does the list represent an endorsement by the author. I do believe that the work shown is representative of the quality of work available today.

Larry Amrine

arry Amrine is both a superb metalsmith and a stockmaker. He has been a full-time maker since 1961. His study of the late Lenard Brownell along with Jerry Fisher's work, combined with the pre-war guns and rifles from London, has left a decisive mark on his work. He prefers to build complete top quality rifles and shotguns and has built everything from practical hunting guns to museum quality exhibition pieces. He works closely with engraver Robert Swartley and toolmaker William Crowley. Amrine does everything in-house except the engraving, case, and accessory tools. To Amrine, a top quality arm is more than just a pretty stock. He believes that it must be a harmonious blend of dynamic handling, balance of line, beauty, and superior functionality.

His stockwork is hand cut from the blank and oil finished. He feels that epoxy and glass are no substitute for careful inletting and does not use synthetic bedding compounds. He works in the classic style and keeps with the theme of the gun. His guns have been used in the hunting fields all over the world. Most of his recent work has been on large bore rifles for the African hunter. He builds complete heavy bore magazine rifles and does restoration work on double rifles.

Dietrich Apel

ietrich Apel, my dear friend of many years running, while not exactly ancient, is a bit long in the tooth. He is one of the few people I know who is older than I am. His coworker at New England Custom Gun Service, Mark Cromwell, is not as old as most of my Levi's. Even so, he is a heck of a gunmaking virtuoso. Apel is Suhl-trained—he grew up in one of Germany's foremost gunmaking families, the Jaegers. He served an apprenticeship under his grandfather, Franz Jaeger. When the Iron Curtain clamped down, he made a narrow escape to the West and went to work for the US Air Force at the Wiesbaden Rod & Gun Club. Later, he went to work with Kurt Jaeger, in a new gun business in Mainz.

In 1952, he immigrated to the US and worked as a gunsmith and stockmaker for his uncle, Paul Jaeger. Bill Ruger offered Apel the opportunity to help with the development of a new shotgun and he moved to New Hampshire to work for Ruger. After his tenure with Ruger, he did custom work from his home shop in New Hampshire. When his uncle offered him the opportunity to continue the Jaeger business, Apel moved back to Jenkintown, Pennsylvania, and ran the company until he sold it in 1986. After that, he returned to New Hampshire and founded the New England Custom Gun Service.

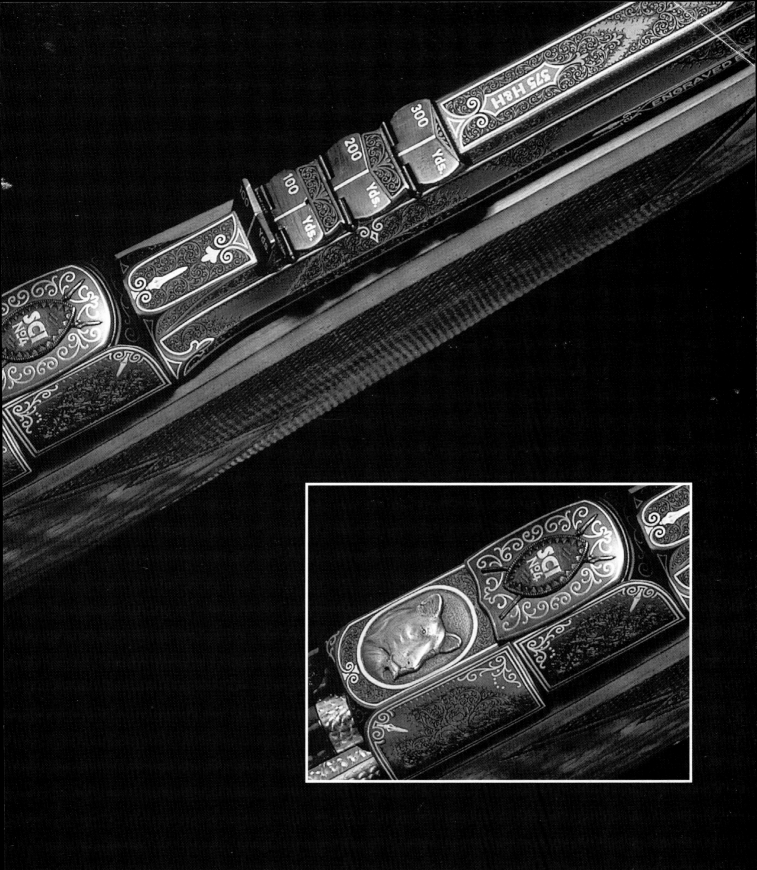

The Lion Rifle was the fourth in the Safari Club International "Guns of the Big Five" series. It was the first to sell at auction for more than $100,000 ($140,000 to be precise). The rifle was built by Paul Jaeger, Inc., then owned by Dietrich Apel. Apel organized and managed the project, but did little of the actual work personally. He could have done so, though. The metalwork was done mostly by Alfred Wyss-Gallifent, the stock by John Mercer, the engraving by Claus Willig, and the accessories by Bill Crowley. Photo courtesy of Safari Club International.

Steve Billeb

ecause of his life-long preoccupation of the outdoors and its inhabitants, Steve Billeb completed Bachelor and Master's degrees in zoology at San Francisco State University with additional graduate work at Penn State and Montana State. His gunmaking grew out of his outdoor-related hobbies. He has been building custom guns professionally since 1974 and did so full time from 1979 until 1990.

While primarily nationally known as a stockmaker, he also does many metalsmithing tasks and likes to oversee as much of the total work as possible in order to coordinate a custom firearm into a unified whole. His specialties are in lightweight sporters and double guns, particularly where styling and components can lend themselves to a particular purpose or theme.

In 1983, Billeb helped found the ACGG and has served as a director, vice president, and president of that organization. In 1990 he joined the teaching staff of Southeastern Community College and has overseen the evolution of the gunsmithing program at that institution. The program emphasizes custom firearms.

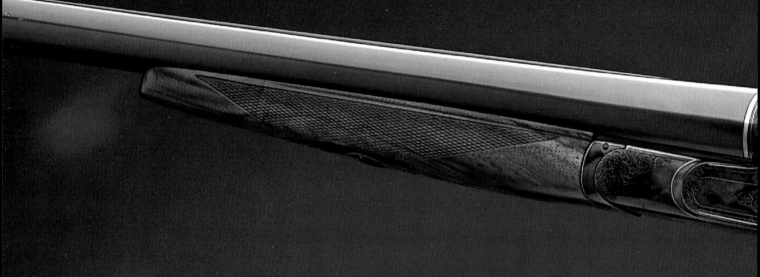

This lovely L.C. Smith custom shotgun is the resultant of the artistry of three men, metalsmith Pete Mazur, stockmaker Steve Billeb, and engraver Bob Evans. As can be seen, all the work on this gun is superb. Billeb's stockwork is particularly noteworthy as L.C. Smith guns are notorious for splitting stocks at the locks. Billeb went to extraordinary lengths to insure that will never happen with this fine gun. Photo by Mustafa Bilal, courtesy of the American Custom Gunmakers Guild.

John Bolliger

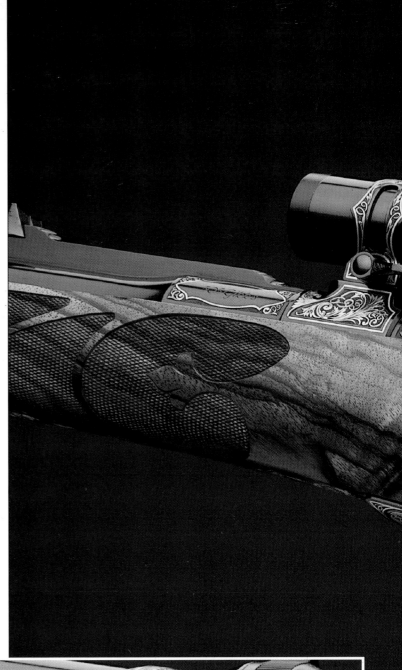

A native Idahoan, John Bolliger began making rifles in 1965 as a hobby. He couldn't afford a custom rifle, but wanted more than a production model, so his only alternative was to build it himself. He soon dedicated himself to producing the highest quality custom rifles he could. He admired and emulated the work of Norm Schiffman, Jerry Fisher, and Dale Goens.

As he struggled in the early years, he eventually developed a following of gun enthusiasts in the local area. This provided him with enough orders to enable him to refine his skills. He reached a plateau after about ten years. He was delivering good work and receiving many compliments from his clients, but, when he began attending national shows and seeing top-quality talent, he realized that he had not yet achieved that level of expertise. He went back to work even harder to reach that next level.

Safari Club International selected Bolliger's Mountain Riflery to build the first and last rifles in Safari Club's series of five rifles dedicated to the dangerous game animals of the world. The first, the Grizzly Rifle, sold at auction for $225,000, and the second, the Elephant Rifle, brought in $165,000.

After the success of the "Guns of the Big Five" series by the Safari Club, a second series was commenced a few years later. Dubbed the "World's Most Dangerous Game" series, John Bolliger's Mountain Riflery was selected to craft the first and last rifles in the series. Shown here is the Elephant Rifle, the final rifle in the series. Photo by Mustafa Bilal.

146

James Corpe

nother fellow Kentuckian, James Corpe began stockmaking at an early age. He learned what he could from books and trial and error experience. He became a part-time stockmaker in 1975 and turned that into a full-time profession in 1982. He prefers to craft his stocks from the blank using quality English walnut. He designs and makes each stock as an individually unique creation. Fine line checkering using shop-made tools and hand-rubbed oil finishes complement each job he does.

Although he has crafted stocks of many different styles, he favors early British stock design with clean, functional lines. Corpe believes that a stock should be trim, easy to carry, and balanced for quick handling. These features are present in all his stocks, whether on a bolt action sporter or a single-shot classic. He believes that today's gunmaker has to be a combination of artist and craftsman to build a firearm that is well made, pleasing to the eye, and a pleasure to own and shoot.

Kentucky stockmaker James Corpe whittled out the magnificent stock for the John Amber Commemorative rifle shown here. It is typical of his exquisite stockwork. Photo by Mustafa Bilal courtesy of the American Custom Gunmakers Guild.

Mark Cromwell

ark Cromwell decided to make gunsmithing a career very early, and after high school, he attended the Pennsylvania Gunsmith School in Pittsburgh. He completed the full gunsmithing curriculum. His first job as a gunsmith was in the shop of Paul Jaeger. In 1985, he moved with the company to Grand Junction, Tennessee, as a part of the sale of the company. During his six years there, he performed a great variety of gunsmithing work, from the simplest repair job to the finest custom work. In 1990, he moved to New Hampshire to join Dietrich Apel and, in 1992, they formed the New England Custom Gun Service.

Cromwell is primarily a metalsmith and a superb one at that. His artistry in metal complements the work of Apel, who is primarily a stockmaker and project organizer.

Young Mark Cromwell did much of the metalwork on the John Amber Commemorative rifle. Of particular note is the custom scope mounting system which Cromwell designed and executed in steel. Although young in years, he is a very talented metalsmith. Photo by Mustafa Bilal courtesy of the American Custom Gunmakers Guild.

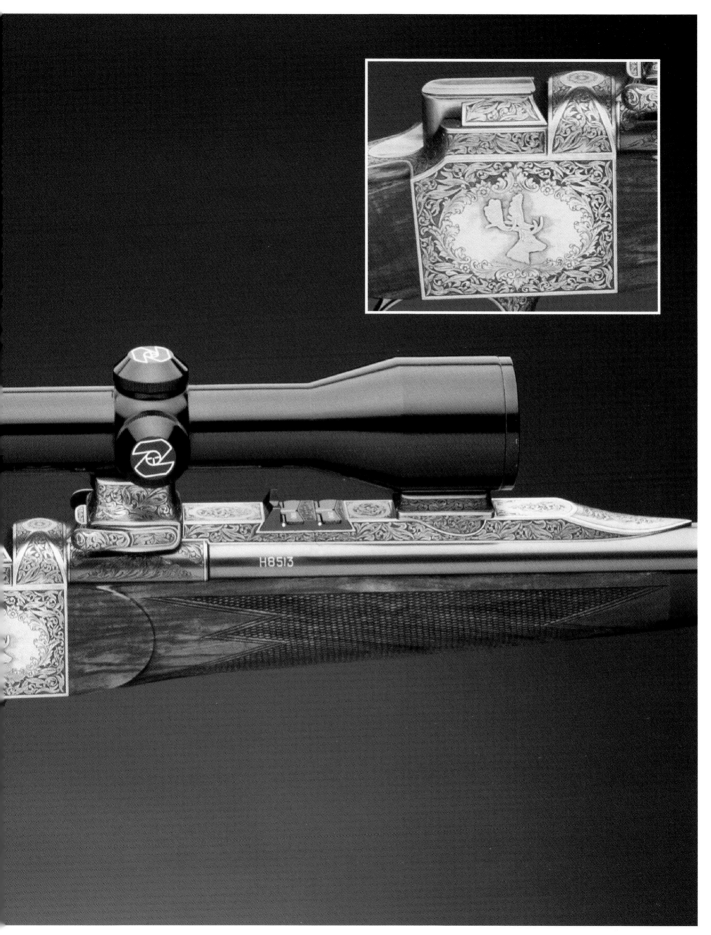

Gary Goudy

A native Californian, Gary Goudy has been crafting exquisite custom stocks for more than thirty years now. Raised on a ranch in Northern California, he contributed to the family larder by supplying the family table with venison, a wild goose, or other assorted game. Guns and hunting were a natural part of his life.

He started tinkering with stocking guns and had the good fortune to meet Joe Oakley in Sacramento where he was living at the time. Oakley took the young aspiring stockmaker into his home and showed him what a classic-styled stock really was. He showed Goudy rifles by Shelhamer, Owen, Brownell, Fisher, Goens, Biesen, and many others. Goudy had never seen such quality work before and was awestruck by it. That experience convinced him that he had a long way to go with his work and he decided to devote all the time it took to learn. He credits Oakley's help and constructive criticisms for much of his success. Added to that, Goudy built a stock for Outdoor Life Shooting Editor, Jim Carmichel, who wrote a story about it. After that story came out in Outdoor Life in 1975, he's been up to his ears in stockwork ever since.

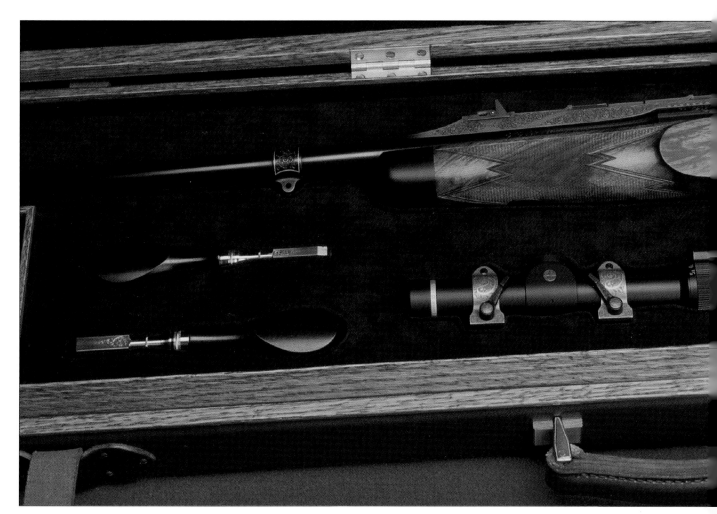

Stockmaker Gary Goudy crafted this wonderful stock for the Ruger No. 1 single-shot rifle. Goudy has been whittling out custom stocks for many years now and is one of the best at it. Photo by Mustafa Bilal courtesy of the American Custom Gunmakers Guild.

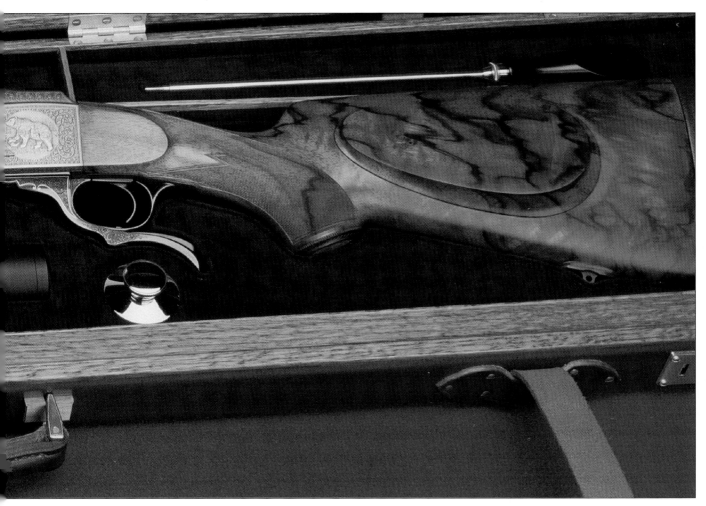

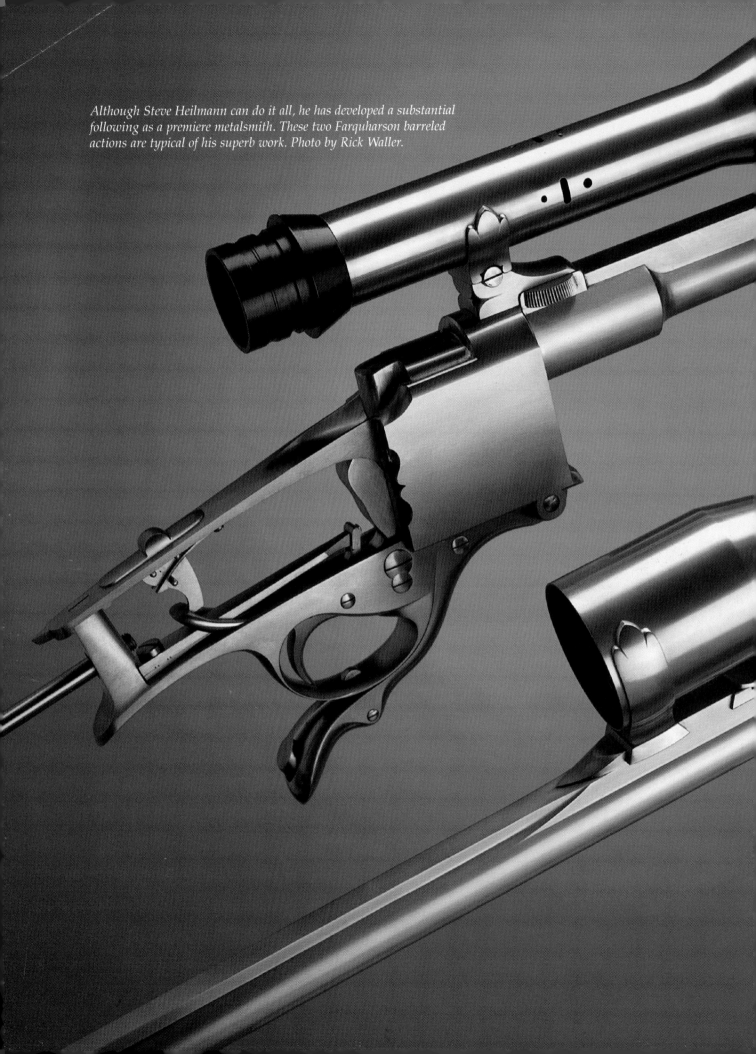

Although Steve Heilmann can do it all, he has developed a substantial following as a premiere metalsmith. These two Farquharson barreled actions are typical of his superb work. Photo by Rick Waller.

Steve Heilmann

$\mathcal{S}$teve Heilmann has been a full-time maker for about twenty-five years since completing the gunsmithing program at the Colorado School of Trades. After he finished his training, he started in the business doing general gunsmithing. He gradually transitioned into stockmaking as his major pursuit and then into metalwork. These days, Heilmann tells me that about 75 percent of his work is devoted to metalsmithing. Heilmann has an enviable reputation among his fellow makers. Much of his metalwork a few years ago was executed for professional stockmakers. Recently, though, private commissions for his artistry in metal have exceeded his work for other professionals.

One of his recent projects, a two gun set consisting of a sidelock double shotgun and a bolt action express rifle, received the prestigious Firearms Marketing Group Award of Excellence. This award, presented annually at the combined FEGA-ACGG Exhibition, is judged by a panel of fellow professionals. Heilmann did all the metal and stockwork on both guns in the set. Steve Heilmann is a fantastic artisan.

Darwin Hensley

L ike most other gunmakers, Hensley has been a hunter since early childhood. As a youngster growing up on a farm in Missouri, he could usually be found either hunting or carving something with his favorite pocket knife. He graduated from college with a degree in fine arts, with his major study area in sculpture. When he graduated, the faculty voted him the outstanding graduating senior artist. He taught art for two years after that. Throughout the years of raising a family, he created various sculpture pieces and produced reproduction antique furniture. Additionally, he restored and repaired antique furniture, which included reproducing carvings.

He is basically self-taught, although he received much encouragement from family and friends. He particularly received a great boost in confidence from Al Lind. He studied various styles through voracious reading and finally decided to combine his training in art with his love for fine guns by crafting gunstocks. He prefers doing bolt action and single-shot rifles.

Hensley is a full-time stockmaker. He designed the stocks for the Kimber Big Game and African series of rifles. Recently, he has stocked many single-shot rifles, particularly of the British Farquharson design.

Darwin Hensley has, in recent years, stocked many single-shot rifles. Among them is this German single-shot. All Hensley's stockwork is first-rate. Photo by Mark Ross courtesy of GUNS magazine.

Keith Heppler

eith Heppler began his career in custom stockmaking on a part-time basis in 1955. He spent most of his time as sales manager for a major tobacco company in addition to raising a family. Since 1977, he has devoted full time to creating classic rifle stocks. His current output is some nine to eleven stocks each year; he uses both solid blanks and profiled stocks to his specifications.

He has no formal training in custom stockmaking. The school of trial and error and the school of hard knocks were his teachers. The base for his stocks is high grade French, English, and Bastogne walnut. His favorite actions are good Model 98 Mausers and pre-64 Model 70 Winchesters.

A wonderful custom rifle from the shop of Keith Heppler. This Winchester Model 70 has received the complete treatment. Photo by Mustafa Bilal.

Steven Dodd Hughes

*S*teve Hughes is one of the few custom makers who won't touch a bolt action hunting rifle. Rather, he concentrates his efforts on single-shot rifles, Fox shotguns, and a few lever actions, mostly .22 rimfires. Steve went into the gunsmithing program at Trinidad State Junior College in 1975 after a fishing boat capsized in Alaska when he was working as a commercial fisherman. One dip in the icy waters was enough to convince him to change occupations. At Trinidad, he completed the basic gunsmithing and advanced gun repair programs. After that, he went to work for Green River Forge in Springfield, Oregon, a firm well-known for its high quality muzzleloading guns, for about two years.

In 1980, he moved all his tools into his garage and began a career as a self-employed custom gunmaker. He extensively researches the history of each project that he undertakes and provides his clients with a full-scale drawing of the gun before any work begins. Throughout his career, Hughes has taken great pains to create unique custom work that fits into a time and place in history without duplicating any specific original gun.

Besides his outstanding gunwork, he is also a gifted writer and an accomplished photographer. He writes a column for Shooting Sportsman magazine and contributes articles and photos to many other periodicals.

Steven Dodd Hughes specializes in unusual commissions. Here is a Marlin Model 39-A .22 rimfire with metal and stockwork by Hughes. I think it is the only custom 39-A I have ever seen. Photo by Steven Dodd Hughes.

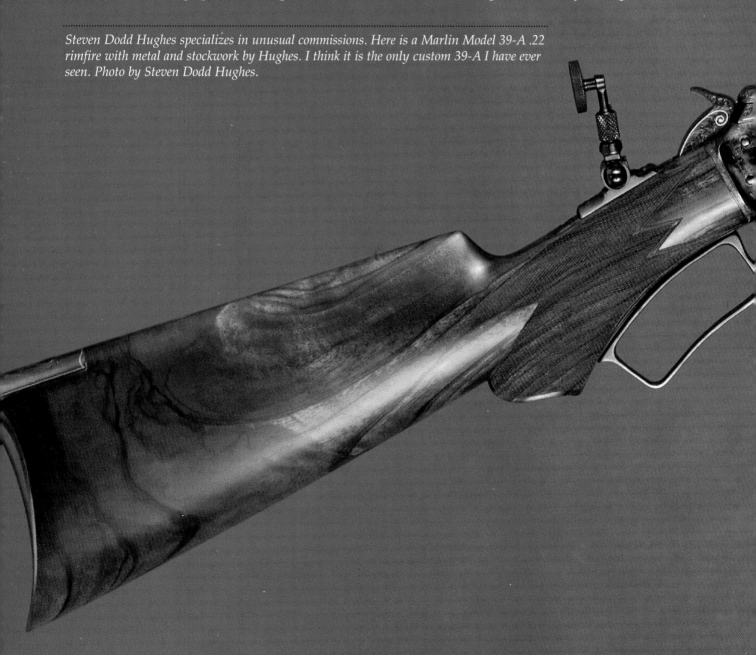

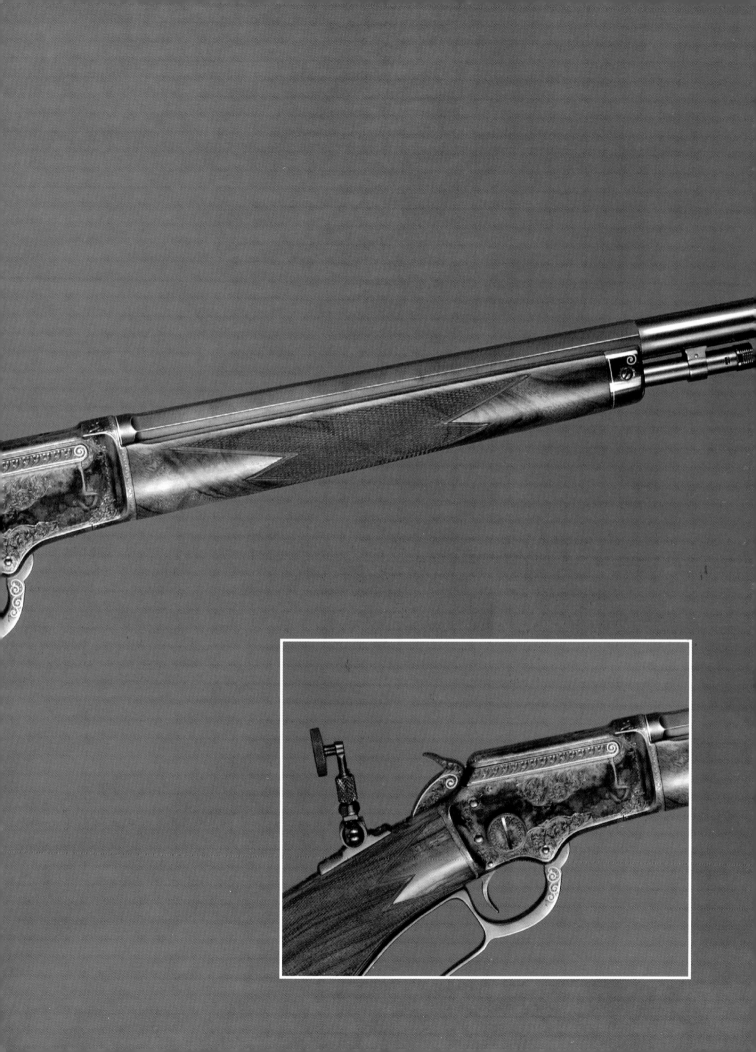

Jay McCament

*J*ay McCament is an outstanding talent who has been able to combine two divergent talents into a multifaceted career. A professional trumpet player and music educator for more than twenty-five years, McCament is now a full-time gunmaker. Under the guidance of his father, he was raised with guns and the shooting sports and his fascination with stockmaking was obvious at an early age.

After college and military service interrupted pursuit of this fascination, he resumed his interest and began making gunstocks on a hobby basis. As he improved his ideas and skills, he transformed his hobby into a consuming life interest. He studied the work of masters in the field and was encouraged by several of them, particularly his good friend, Al Lind. McCament has become a dedicated practitioner in the pursuit of excellence in custom gunmaking. He executes both splendid metalwork and stockwork, and shows no preference of one over the other. He believes that the elegant simplicity of the classic style emphasizes the refinement of all components and their assimilation into an artistic and functional whole. Jay McCament builds one heck of a nice rifle.

A pair of rifles from the shop of Jay McCament. McCament did all the metal and stockwork on this matching pair of rifles. Bob Evans did the unusual southwestern-style engraving. Photo by Mustafa Bilal.

The David Miller Company

This renowned company consists of two fantastic artisans, David Miller and Curt Crum. Although either master can do it all when it comes to crafting a custom rifle of the highest quality, Miller executes mostly metalwork and Crum handles the stockmaking chores. I have spent many hours in the Miller shop and if there is a better organized one out there, I have yet to see it. Each and every tool in the shop has its place and if not in use at any given point in time, it is in its assigned place. In my small amateur shop, I spend far more time looking for something than I do getting a task done!

The top-end custom rifles that come from the Miller shop are arguably the best available—certainly, I don't believe that anyone would debate categorizing the Miller rifle as one of the very best. Alas, it is also the most expensive custom rifle that I know of. Recently, however, the Miller shop has come out with a less costly rifle called the Marksman. Until its development, the shop produced but one grade—the "spare no effort" model. The Marksman is designed for flawless operation and long-range accuracy potential. It is intended to be a hunting rifle instead of an instant collectors item. As such, it lacks some of the frills of the top-end rifle, but the craftsmanship going into both models is the same. Miller was raised in Indiana and Crum in Colorado, but both have long since converted into Arizonans.

Tucson gunmakers David Miller and Curt Crum of the David Miller Co. turned out this exquisite rifle. Their rifle represents the epitome of quality in a custom gun. Photo by Ron Dehn.

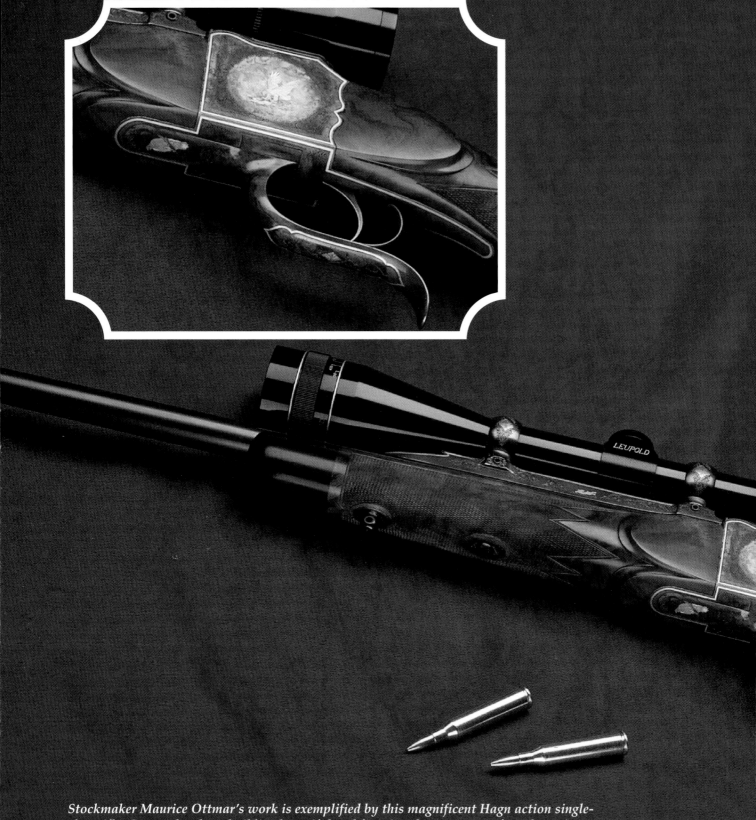

Stockmaker Maurice Ottmar's work is exemplified by this magnificent Hagn action single-shot rifle. Ottmar has been building beautiful and functional custom guns for a long time. The engraving was executed by Terry Wallace. Photo by Gary Bolster.

Maurice Ottmar

aurice Ottmar began gunsmithing as a hobby while he ran a wheat and cattle ranch in Washington. Because he enjoyed gunwork more than ranching, he signed up for the Trinidad State Junior College Gunsmithing Program. After graduation, he went to work for Champlin Firearms in Enid, Oklahoma, as a stockmaker in 1972. After a couple years in the shop in Enid, he returned to his hometown, Coulee City, where he continues to do Champlin stocks as well as stocks and complete rifles of his own. He is a full-time maker.

Ottmar has the equipment and ability to do the metalwork necessary for a complete rifle. He does barreling, polishing, sight work, cold rust bluing, and many other metalsmithing tasks. His preference is for bolt rifles in the medium caliber range, but also builds the occasional shotgun, double rifle, and single-shot. His favorite checkering patterns are the point, broken point, and his version of Dale Goens' O'Connor pattern, but he does more fleur-de-lis patterns than the others. He works in the classic style and he does not use semi-inlets or a pantograph; he makes all his stocks from the blank.

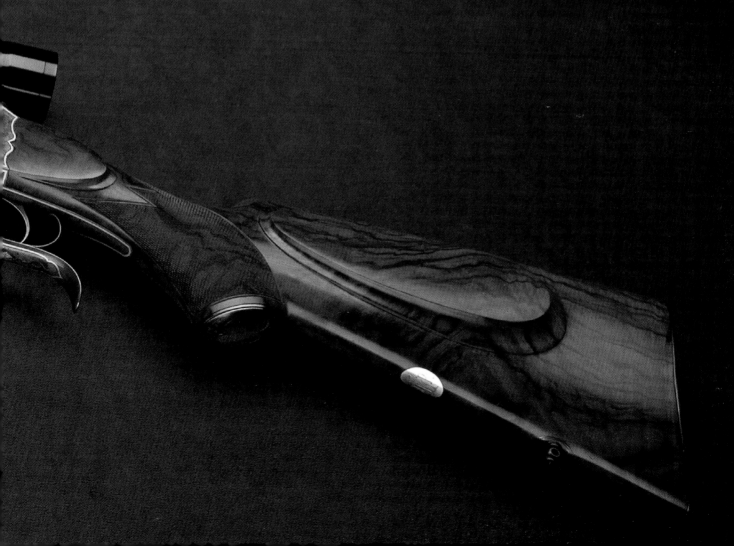

Bruce Russell

B ruce Russell is a superbly talented gunmaker whom I have never met. I first learned of him and his work in a discussion with Steve Dodd Hughes where Hughes described his skills in almost superhuman terms. When a fellow gunmaker characterizes the work of another in those terms, believe me, I listen. I know of no higher compliment for a gunmaker than to have one of his peers praise his work. Hughes, also an excellent photographer, sent me several photos of Russell's work. I was duly impressed.

Russell is a craftsman who knows nothing but the best and anything less than his best effort is unacceptable on any job. He is also multifaceted in that he is equally at home when he works on bolt action rifles or double shotguns, and can do both outstanding metalwork and stockwork. Although the vast majority of his work is pure classic, he will also do an occasional job that is not.

....

Wyoming maker Bruce Russell did both the metal and stockwork on this Mauser action sporter. Russell's work is clean, crisp, and uniformly excellent. Photo by Steven Dodd Hughes.

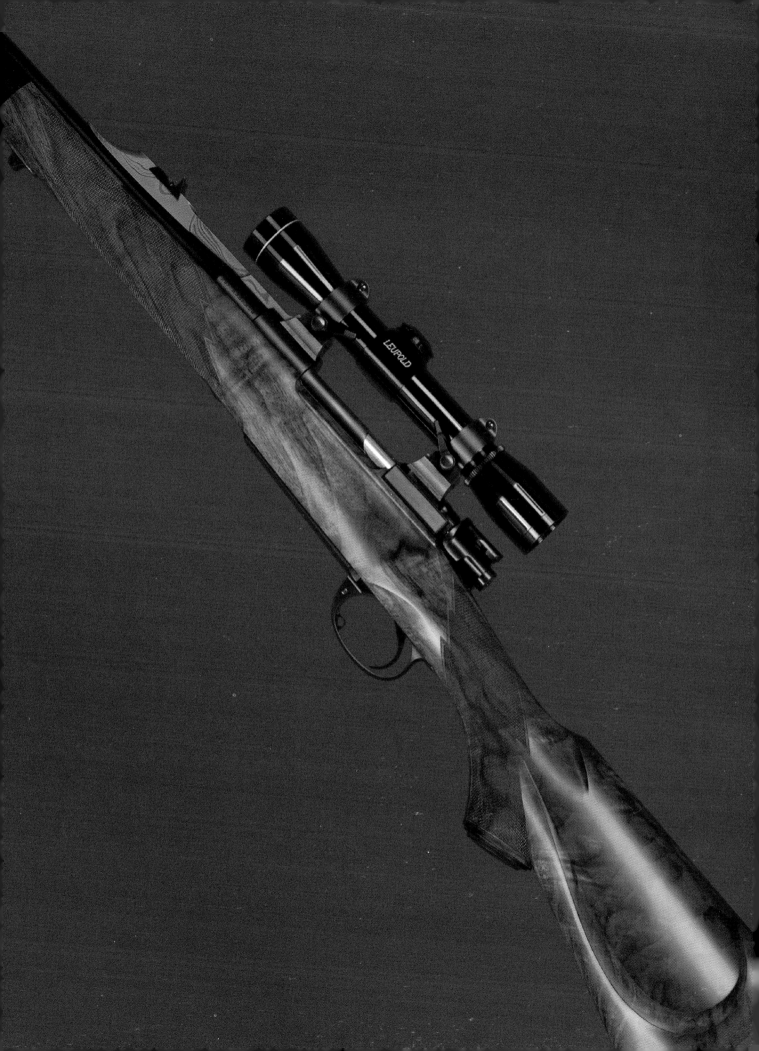

Bill Simen

I first learned of Bill Simmen while doing a magazine article on the work of Gary Stiles. Stiles sent me a takedown switch barrel rifle he had built. Not only was I impressed with his metalwork, but I also found the stockwork to be exquisite. When I asked him who had made the stock, he told me that a fellow native Pennsylvanian, Bill Simmen, had done it.

Simmen always liked guns and got into the business after he bought a production muzzleloader to use for Pennsylvania's deer season. He quickly outgrew the lack of quality and sophistication of the production gun. He decided to build an authentic long rifle and, as they say, the rest is history. He enjoyed a part-time career building muzzleloaders and an occasional centerfire rifle while working at a Volkswagen factory. When the corporate staff of VW decided to close the plant, Simmen found himself out of a job.

He then attended the Pittsburgh Gunsmithing School and after graduation he worked with a couple local gunsmiths for about a year. As his clientele grew, he went to full-time gunmaker status, which included restoration work. He still crafts many muzzleloaders, but centerfire work now comprises more than half his time.

Gunmaker Bill Simmen turned this Heym-Ruger into a lovely rifle. It was previously stocked in a Germanic hogs-back Bavarian style which gave me chills and fever every time I looked at it. The stock is now a fitting addition to the otherwise excellent quality of the rifle.

Long-time maker Bob Snapp has, in recent years, specialized in single-shot rifles. This Winchester High Wall is a good example of his virtuosity in metal. His metalwork on this rifle was extensive. The stock was crafted by James Tucker. Photo by Steven Dodd Hughes.

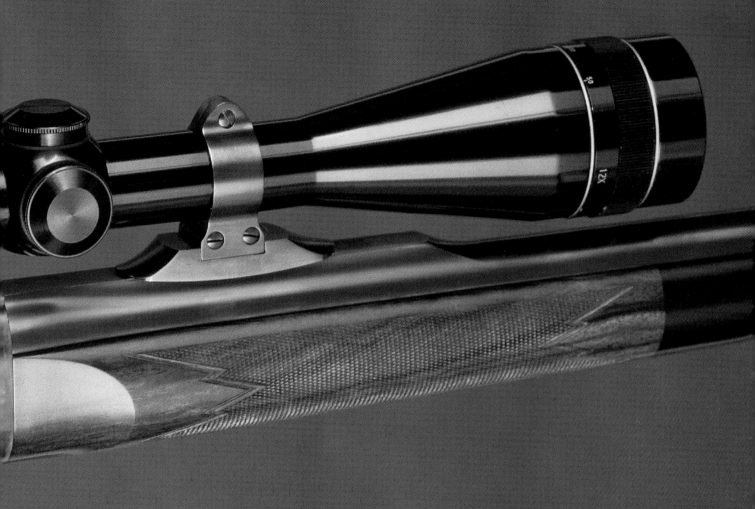

Bob Snapp

ob Snapp is the son of an avid hunter and the grandson of a professional market hunter (during the era when market hunting was a legal profession). Naturally, he was interested in firearms. He graduated in gunsmithing from Trinidad State Junior College in 1951. At that time, P.O. Ackley and Bob West were still teaching there. Since then, he has pretty much been at it on a full-time basis. For many years he specialized in rifle barrel work, chambering for 1,000 different rifle and pistol cartridges. He did rebarreling, rechambering, reboring, relining, and caliber conversions for a long time. Gradually, more and more single-shot rifle work came in and for the past five years or so, nothing but single-shot rifles. He does execute an occasional special project, but other than that, he does strictly single-shots. He is semi-retired now which means, as he related to me, he accepts only those commissions he wants to do. That means top quality single-shot rifles only.

Snapp is the past president and past secretary of the ACGG.

Gary Stiles

A native of Homer City, Pennsylvania, Gary Stiles has spent all of his life in that area. He studied electronics at Greenburg Institute of Technology and then went to work at a manufacturing plant as an apprentice machinist. He left after five years when he had learned all he could about the trade and opened a heavy equipment repair and rebuilding business. Hunting came naturally to him and he reworked several of his personal firearms to add refinements. He did such things as redesigning safeties and rebarreling actions. Several of his friends saw what he had done and began asking him to work on their firearms. Before he knew it, he was working many hours each week in gunsmithing in addition to his other business.

Stiles performs all facets of gunmaking. His most recent project is building a side-by-side double rifle. He also converts rifles to takedown, switch barrel models. I had one of these rifles he had built, with one .35 Whelen barrel, and a second in .25-06. The rifle had a Mauser action and it functioned flawlessly. It was also surprisingly accurate for a takedown model. He enjoys working with his clients and will try to accommodate most any wish they have.

Quaker State native Gary Stiles turned out this excellent switch barrel rifle. With barrel sets for the .35 Whelen and .25-06, it pretty well covers any hunting situation in North America. Bill Simmen stocked the rifle. Photo by Mark Ross courtesy of GUNS magazine.

Stockmaker James Tucker crafted the wonderful stock on this Winchester High Wall. Tucker had his shop in California for a number of years but recently moved it to New Hampshire. Photo by Steven Dodd Hughes.

James C. Tucker

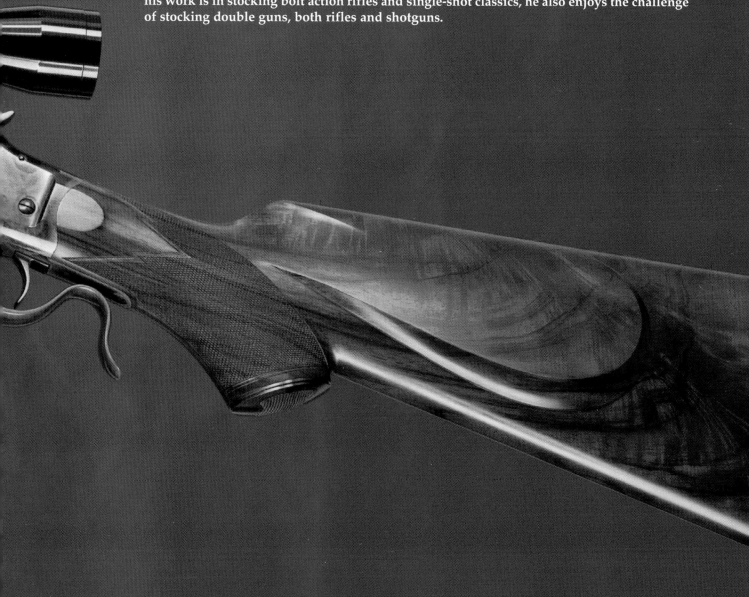

ucker was introduced to gunsmithing by his high school machine shop instructor. Following his graduation in 1975, he enrolled in the gunsmithing program at Lassen Junior College where he completed the two year course, and graduated with an AA degree. He moved around a bit after that and worked for both Weatherby as a custom stockmaker for about a year and then for Paul Jaeger, Inc. for about three years. He then returned to his native state of California and has been self-employed since that time. Recently, he moved to New Hampshire where he currently resides and works.

He credits many people who helped him along the way in the development of his skills, but singles out two in particular, John Hearn and Alfred Wyss-Gallifent. Both were fellow employees while he was with Jaeger. Hearn, a long time stockmaker, taught him the techniques of final shaping and simplicity of design while Wyss-Gallifent taught him the basics of stocking double guns. Both, and many others, taught him craftsmanship. Though much of his work is in stocking bolt action rifles and single-shot classics, he also enjoys the challenge of stocking double guns, both rifles and shotguns.

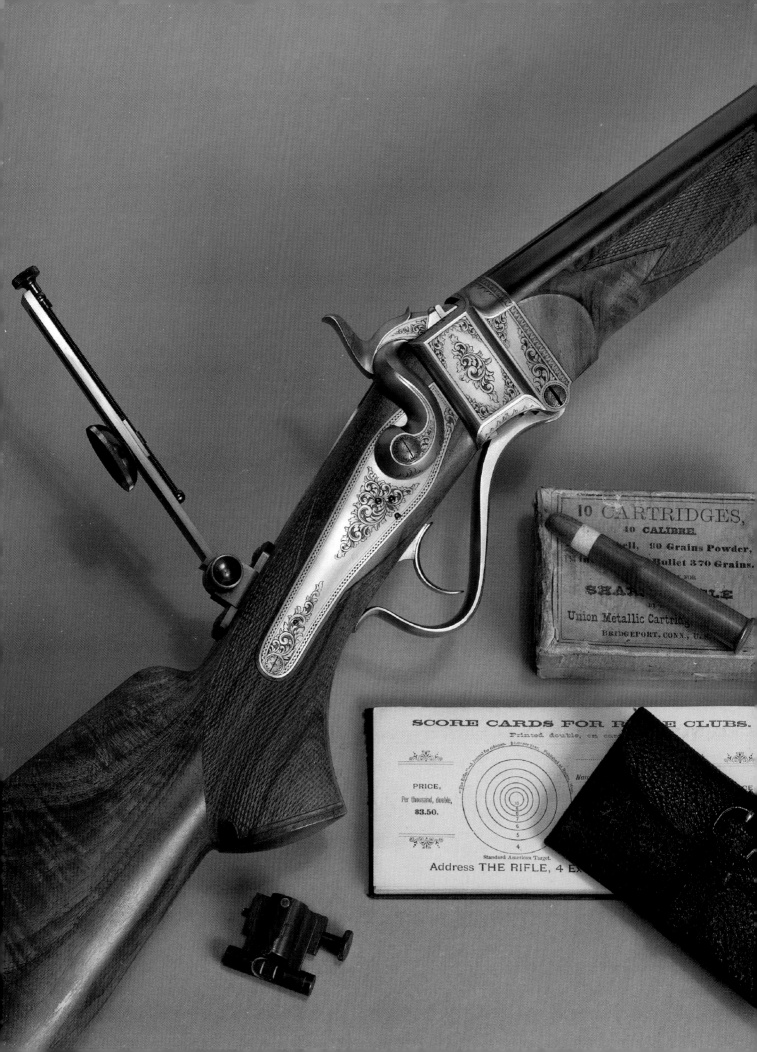

Ed Webber

A Montanan, Ed Webber was raised on a cattle ranch in the Big Sky country. He has a Bachelor's Degree and has completed post graduate work in art, with minors in history and agriculture. He built custom firearms part-time for several years prior to 1979 when he ceased ranching to concentrate on rifle building. His work largely reflects his primary interest in traditional single-shot sporting rifles, but not exclusively. He also believes that aesthetics are equally as important as craftsmanship and that top quality firearms are a viable fine art form and are functional objects.

Webber's skills are primarily self-taught, yet he credits much of his ability to criticism, advice, and support of his friends in the trade. He started by building muzzleloaders; he made all the parts because he was not satisfied with those that were commercially available. For awhile, he manufactured '77 Sharps models from scratch. He now works only with original parts, though. He also does substantial numbers of restorations. Ed Webber is a top quality craftsman.

Ed Webber likes Sharps and Winchester rifles and does impeccable work on them. This M-77 Sharps is an example. The rifle was engraved by Lynton McKenzie. Photo by Steven Dodd Hughes.

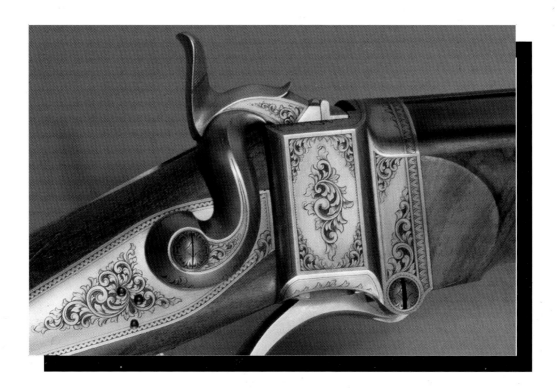

Frank Wells

Frank Wells, although a native of Massachusetts, is now a converted Arizonan. He worked for many years in the retail firearms business as well as in general gunsmithing. He would build the occasional custom rifle as a part of his general gunsmithing, and gradually began specializing in that aspect of the business. During these years, he, in conjunction with old timer Roy Dunlap, developed a silhouette rifle stock that is a standard today. As his clientele developed, he moved more and more away from repairs and general gunsmithing and began building complete rifles instead. For several years, he offered a semi-custom model for the African hunter that was very well made and inexpensively priced. The model was very popular.

These days, though, he does primarily only complete, best quality rifles. He was selected to build the third in the SCI five rifle series which commemorates the dangerous game animals of the world. His rifle was the Lion and Buffalo Rifle. Frank did all the work on the rifle in-house, with the exception of the engraving. The rifle sold at auction for $105,000. Frank says that the SCI gun was his best so far, but he wants to surpass it. Besides being a top quality craftsman, Wells is also a heck of a nice guy.

A Frank Wells version of a Ladies Rifle. Starting with a Sako action, Wells did all the metal and stockwork on this lovely petite rifle. Ken Warren did the engraving. Photo by Ron Dehn.

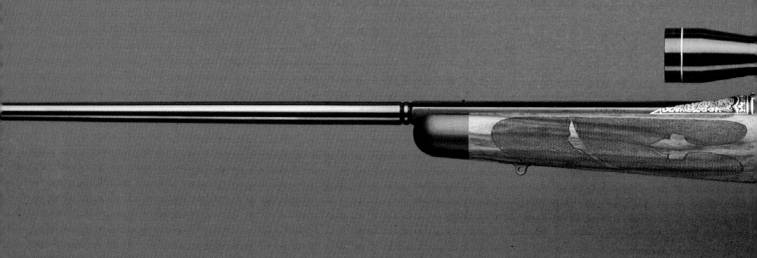

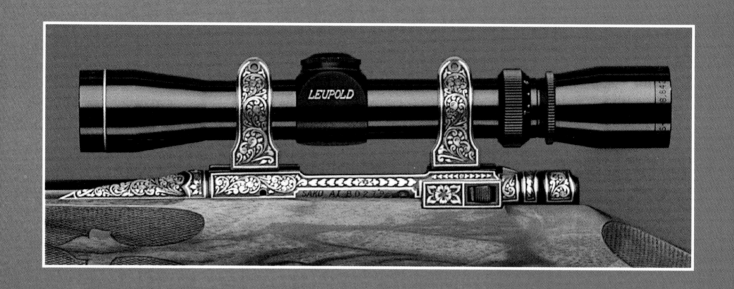

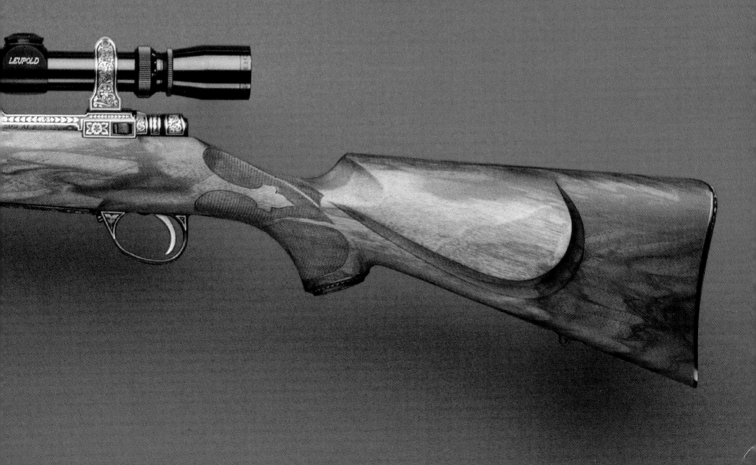

Chapter 12

The Custom Guilds

For many years, there was no organization devoted specifically to the custom gun industry. Most makers and engravers were members of the National Rifle Association, but the NRA, good as it was and is, was a broad-based organization that worked for the benefit of all firearms. The NRA is necessary and all firearm enthusiasts should be members. Still, the custom industry felt more was needed to represent the interests of its specialized segment of the industry.

One champion of this philosophy was the late John T. Amber. The editor of *Gun Digest* for more than thirty years, Amber used this forum to nudge the custom gun industry to the forefront of his readers. Every issue of the book contained a photographic section on custom guns and custom engraving. Without fail, this is the section of the book that I turned to first when a new issue came out. Apparently, many

This unique double rifle is built on a Winchester Model 21 action. Metalsmith Tony Fleming did all the metalwork, Paul Dressel, Jr. did the stock, and Ralph Bone executed the engraving. This rifle was the 11th annual ACGG raffle rifle for the Exhibition held in 1995. Photo by Mustafa Bilal.

The #9 ACGG rifle was put together by the team of metalsmith Jack Belk, stockmaker Maurice Ottmar, and engraver Eric Gold. It is unusual in that it is styled after the British Express rifle, but scaled down to a size appropriate for the .22 long rifle cartridge. Photo by Steven Dodd Hughes.

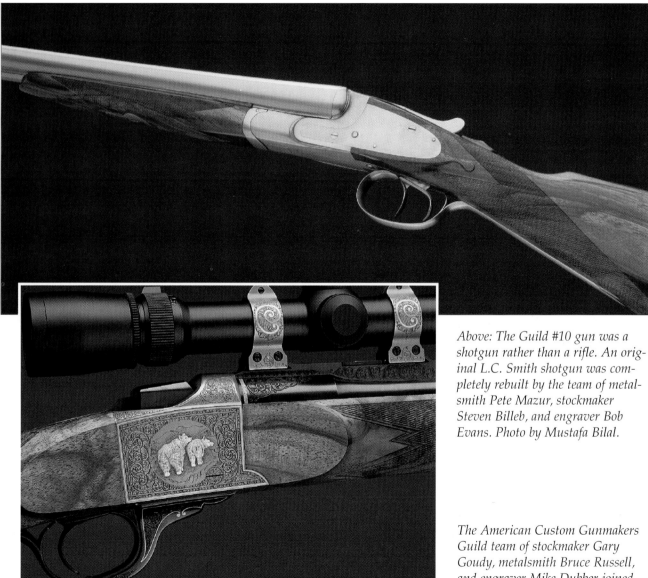

Above: The Guild #10 gun was a shotgun rather than a rifle. An original L.C. Smith shotgun was completely rebuilt by the team of metalsmith Pete Mazur, stockmaker Steven Billeb, and engraver Bob Evans. Photo by Mustafa Bilal.

The American Custom Gunmakers Guild team of stockmaker Gary Goudy, metalsmith Bruce Russell, and engraver Mike Dubber joined forces to craft the ACGG #8 rifle. Photo by Mustafa Bilal.

This Model 71 Winchester has been adorned with the superb engraving of New Yorker Marty Rabeno. Marty's combination of scrollwork and bulino engraving is superb. Photo courtesy of the Firearms Engravers Guild of America.

The latest in the series of raffle sets by the American Custom Gunmakers Guild is this Gentlemen's Set by the team of metalsmith Bob Snapp, stockmaker Steven Dodd Hughes, and engraver Frank Hendricks. The set replicates turn-of-the-century target guns. Photo by Mustafa Bilal.

readers did the same because the section seemed to expand each and every year.

In addition, almost every issue of the book contained a feature article or two on the subject. Most were penned by the editor himself. He had many friends in the industry and usually had several personal custom jobs on order. It was a rare issue that he didn't report on the custom deliveries he had received during the year. It was from his writings that I first learned of many craftsmen in the field and saw photo coverage of their work. Later, when I got to know Amber well, he introduced me to many of them. John Amber was the custom gunmaker and engraver's best friend.

The gun engravers were the first to organize. In June 1980, twenty-one engravers from across the country met in Las Vegas. This informal meeting was the catalyst for the formation of the Firearms Engravers Guild of America (FEGA). The group met again the following year in Houston where thirty-five engravers formally voted to guild into existence. Bylaws were adopted and FEGA was incorporated (not for profit) in the state of Texas.

The established objectives of FEGA are to provide opportunities for engravers to exchange ideas and knowledge, assist in improving individual skills, promote firearms engraving as a legitimate art form, and to raise public interest and appreciation in quality firearms engraving.

Since that formation, the guild has become the recognized source of information on American engravers and engraving. It has drastically raised the level of recognition of the art. The camaraderie of its members and the resulting exchange of artistic and ethical thought has inspired unprecedented interest in the art form. Before the founding of the guild, American engravers were generally thought, with a few exceptions, to lag several orders of magnitude behind their European counterparts in talent and skill. The development of the guild had much to do with turning that ill-founded idea around.

With the engravers guild a reality, the custom makers were not far behind. The American Custom Gunmakers Guild (ACGG) came into existence in 1983 at the NRA convention in Phoenix. Seventy-six charter members joined at that time. The ACGG is also incorporated as a non-profit organization. The guild grew out of the minds of two men, Steve Billeb

and John Maxon. They surveyed their peers in the industry and found common interest and support in the proposal.

The purpose of the ACGG is to be a viable association of craftsmen who are actively engaged in the art of custom gunmaking, stockmaking, metalsmithing, engraving, and other related specialties. The guild promotes the exchange of ideas and techniques and strives to promote public interest and awareness in the craft. The intent is to advance the cause and betterment of custom gunmaking as an accepted art form.

The ACGG strives to promote standards of excellence and, to this end, acceptance for regular membership is only after submitting work for inspection and acceptance at the annual meeting by current reg-

Two unusual custom jobs: The top gun is a 1890 Deluxe Winchester pump stocked by Darwin Hensley and engraved by Bob Evans. The bottom gun is a Model 63 Winchester semi-auto .22 stocked by Jay McCament and also engraved by Bob Evans. Photo courtesy of the Firearms Engravers Guild of America.

Steve Heilmann did all the metal and stockwork on this British-style Express rifle. The stylish engraving was executed by Terry Wallace. Both did magnificent work. Photo by Rick Waller.

ular members present. High ethical standards are mandatory and an ethics committee was mandated by the bylaws for the sole purpose of resolving disputes and hopefully preventing legitimate complaints.

In 1985, FEGA and the ACGG joined forces to produce the annual Custom Gunmakers and Engravers Exhibition. This exhibition is the greatest assembly of custom guns and engraving in America. The gathering is also used to conduct educational seminars and necessary annual business meetings, as well as recognize individual and group achievement with an awards program. Each guild also publishes its own journal periodically and uses the publication to pass along news and provide educational tips from the membership. Each guild also produces video tapes on various aspects of their art and make them available for a nominal fee.

There are, of course, very talented artisans, both engravers and gunmakers, who are not members of either guild. Their reasons are as varied as their personalities. Some are such individualists that they simply prefer to stand alone. Others have political arguments with the guilds and remain out for that reason. Some, I suppose, feel that they have succeeded very nicely without membership in such a professional organization and see no advantage to becoming a member. Artisans don't join the guilds for the same reasons that other people don't join the Elks, Moose, or Boy Scouts for that matter.

Still, the ACGG has, including associates, about 300 members. FEGA has a few less with about 250 members. FEGA makes no distinction between regular and associate membership. Any interested individual can join. Of this total number, perhaps half are actively involved in the business. It might even be somewhat less that half. The remainder are friends of the art or are perfecting their skills to apply for regular membership. How many nonmembers who are out there practicing their art I can't say, but would guess at least an equal number.

The two guilds have done much to promote awareness in all aspects of custom gunmaking. The obvious increase in the general quality of custom guns today as compared to only a few short years ago is due largely to the existence of the guilds. Old John knew what he was doing when he goaded and prodded various artisans into getting together with the idea of a guild in mind. Every aspect of the crafting of custom guns has dramatically improved as a result.

Chapter 13

Factory Custom Guns

nother option to ordering a full custom rifle from one of the many makers, is to contact either the Remington or United States Repeating Arms Company (USRAC) custom shop. Both these makers maintain custom shops to satisfy special needs of some of their customers and have done so for many years. At one time, Roy Weatherby maintained a custom shop of sorts as well, but I don't believe that is the case today. Ruger has never had a custom shop—the decision was quickly made in the company not to develop a custom shop.

Several of the European manufacturers also do custom work to order, but don't maintain a custom shop per se. Most European plants employ more handwork in their production anyway, so adding custom features is not difficult within their normal work force. For particularly exquisite features, such as extensive engraving, they often employ outside artisans on a sub-contract basis. Standard engraving patterns are normally executed by in-house personnel.

There are a few manufacturers that are nothing but a custom shop. I am thinking of such distinguished firms as Purdey, Holland & Holland, Boss, and Hartmann & Weiss. Referring to such firms as a manufacturer is probably a misnomer in the first place. At one time, Purdey, H&H, and

several of the other London makers did offer a standard model or two for sale. I don't believe they do that anymore and accept clients only on a special order basis. If that is the case, they would really be much more of a custom shop operation than a manufacturer.

I am familiar with the operation of a small German manufacturer, F.W. Heym. Most European manufacturers are similar in their operations and the way Heym does things would be, I think, representative of the others. Heym offers a standard line of firearms to the trade. It has a bolt

Alas, the custom shop of Symes & Wright is no longer in business. While it was, though, its best quality guns were superb. Made in the London tradition, they were every bit the equal of the older and more famous makers. Photo courtesy of Symes & Wright.

187

action hunting rifle, a double rifle in both side by side, and over/under versions plus a variety of combination guns.

The closest thing to a mass-produced firearm it offers is the bolt action SR-20 hunting rifle. Even it, though, has considerable handwork involved in its construction. A customer can order special wood, special stock dimensions, barrel lengths, sights, and other relatively minor changes, all at extra cost, of course. A wide variety of engraving patterns can also be ordered. The simpler jobs are executed by in-house engravers, but a major work would be sub-contracted out to one of several master engravers.

The doubles and combination guns are available in standard models, each almost exactly like the next. Options

are also available on these models. Much handwork goes into their construction anyway, much more so than the repeaters. Perhaps the most elaborate gun Heym has ever built was put together in the mid-80s. It was the third rifle in SCI's Guns of the Big Five series and commemorated the Cape buffalo. Heym chose to produce an elegant sidelock double rifle as its effort. I believe it was probably the finest gun Heym has ever built—certainly in recent times anyway. The gun was sold at auction in, I believe 1984, for $65,000. I think that was a record price for a modern firearm at the time. It has been surpassed several times since then though, and by very large amounts.

An over/under shotgun from the London shop of Symes & Wright. This small English company set up shop to compete with the famous London makers for the best quality trade. Unfortunately, although the quality of the product was outstanding, the company is no longer in business. Photo courtesy of Symes & Wright.

Although the German manufacturer F.W. Heym doesn't have a custom shop per se, it does produce custom quality pieces. This Model 88B Safari is a sidelock double rifle and was the Buffalo Rifle in the Safari Club "Guns of the Big Five" series. Photo courtesy of F.W. Heym.

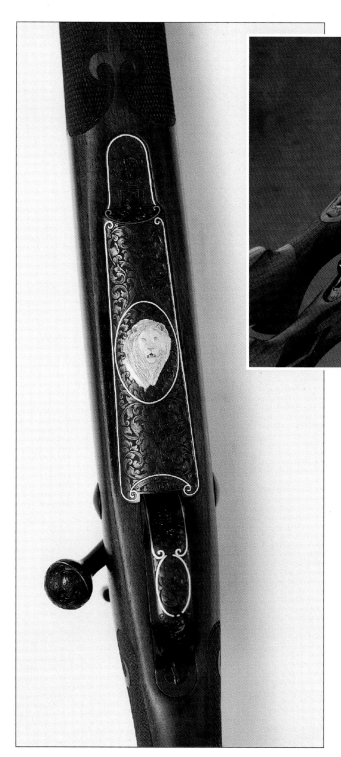

Winchester also maintains a custom shop as it has from the beginning. This Model 70 is an example of its custom shop output. Photo courtesy of US Repeating Arms Co.

When USRAC took over the firearms manufacturing division of Winchester, it retained the rights to use the Winchester name and logo and it preserved the Winchester custom shop. The fortunes of the new company USRAC, with the old product name, Winchester, were pretty rocky for several years, though. That is a fact that was not limited to USRAC either. Most of the industry had a very difficult

Factory custom shops have been around for eons now. Shown here are two examples from the Remington Custom Shop. Photo courtesy of the Remington Arms Company.

time. Many old and well-know names fell by the wayside. Others, equally respected, hung on by the skin of their teeth.

As Olin had done with Winchester firearms, DuPont divested itself of Remington by selling the company to an investment group. USRAC and Browning were finally bought by a French consortium and some much needed capital was invested in their operations. These days, they seem to be doing fine. Remington also has apparently done well. Ruger, as best I can tell, weathered the period best of all.

Through it all, both USRAC and Remington maintained their custom shops. The Remington custom shop is pretty complete with specialists in all aspects of crafting a firearm, including a couple engravers. These artisans are all Remington employees—I think the total number is about nineteen or so. USRAC, on the other hand, relies a bit more than does Remington on outside independent craftsmen to perform at least some of the tasks from its custom shop. Of course, there is nothing wrong with either approach. Many highly reputable firms rely considerably on independent artisans to accomplish work on their top end products.

Remington's custom shop goes back to the founding of the company. When Eliphalet Remington started making firearms in 1816, each one was individually crafted for the customer with no two precisely alike. Whatever the customer wanted, he got. Remington did not limit his production for his customers to merely aesthetics either. His major goal was to produce a firearm for his customers that functioned and shot as good as it looked. It was his reputation

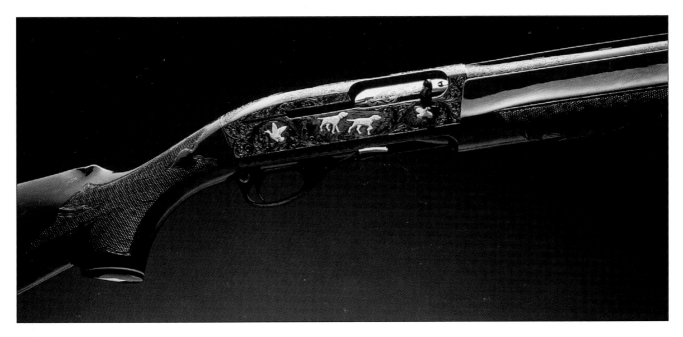

The Remington Custom Shop also turns out custom shotguns. This "F" Grade Model 11-87 is an example of its custom shotguns. Photo courtesy of Remington Arms Co.

for building fine, individually built guns that pushed Remington into the production gun business later on.

Since that beginning, the custom shop has continually played a very important role in the Remington production and its growth. Several production guns can trace their roots to the work of the custom shop, both in design and in functional improvements. The custom shop continues to do just that today and has done so for about 175 years now.

The major differences in the products of the custom shops and the regular production pieces can be summed up in one word—handwork. Both USRAC and Remington start with factory-produced parts, the same parts that will eventually end up in production guns. The big difference is that the custom shops draw their components very early in the production process. Each then brings the components into the custom shop and the handwork begins. Actions are trued, hand honed, and polished until every part functions as a unit. Remington draws its barrels as blanks with only the boring and rifling completed. The remainder of the barrel work—profiling, chambering, threading, polishing, and finishing—is done one barrel at a time.

USRAC, on the other hand, uses selected production barrels for its work unless a match grade barrel is specified on the order. In that case, the barrel work is performed by an outside contractor with a reputation for the highest quality precision barrel work.

Actions are selected for each custom shop while in their annealed state. This eases the task of preparing the action considerably. If engraving is on the order, it is also engraved before being properly tempered. Both shops offer a wide variety of options to enable the customer to personalize his bolt action rifle. Remington will also do custom work on its shotguns as well as its pump action and semi-auto rifles.

The USRAC shop does no work on shotguns.

Smith & Wesson had a factory custom shop for many years, but no longer provides this service. It does have a specialty shop that functions much like a custom shop; however, this facility specializes in turning out special models in limited numbers. This shop will turn out from a few hundred to perhaps a thousand limited edition models.

Colt, on the other hand, still maintains its custom shop. With the company's long history, it has provided a custom shop almost from the beginning. Colt still offers this service today.

Naturally, the prices for products from any custom shop are considerably higher than the production firearms, as well they should be. Much of the price differences is attributed to the handwork employed in the crafting of the customers personalized firearm. Higher grades of wood cost more, of course. So do the array of optional features available from either shop. Still, the prices are, in general, well below the cost of a full-blown custom job from an individual maker. Prices are more similar to those of the semi-custom makers.

Do the factory custom shops offer a good value for the dollar invested? I certainly think that they do. They also offer the prospective customer another avenue to obtain a specialized and personalized firearm and at a reasonable cost.

Chapter 14

In Between—Semi-Custom Guns

In Chapter 1, I attempted to define the term Custom Gun. While I'm satisfied with the definition, the reality is that a custom gun is whatever an individual wants it to be. Semi-custom, on the other hand, is somewhere between the standard factory product and the full-blown custom job. Many are produced that are, in most ways, very similar to a custom order. They are largely machine made, but still have enough handwork involved to permit tailoring the product to individual wants and needs, within limits. Large numbers of options are usually offered, at extra cost of course, to permit this tailoring.

The semi-custom maker will turn out several stocks on duplicating machines with just enough excess wood to permit some tailoring. It will then go to one of several stockmakers, Dakota Arms has six or so, who fits it to the metal and brings it to final dimensions. It then goes to the finishing department and after that, to one of perhaps three or four specialists for a checkering job. All other aspects of the job, barreling, polishing, bluing, etc., are similarly done. On most full custom jobs, one artisan does it all. Some semi-custom operations will turn out several guns each day. The custom maker finishes one every month or so, and perhaps even less.

Probably the best example of a semi-custom gun on the market today, and the one that I am personally most familiar with, is produced by Dakota Arms. I do not mean this chapter to be a commercial for Dakota because it does not need my help. I will key on its operation, though, because I am far more knowledgeable about what it does and how it does it—I

Perhaps the best known of the semi-custom gun producers is Dakota Arms. Shown here is an assortment of rifles available over-the-counter from Dakota. Photo courtesy of Dakota Arms.

The newest model from Dakota Arms is the double shotgun model. Available in three versions, this one is the Legend, a top-of-the-line product.

am sure that other like operations are very similar.

Dakota Arms was founded by two superb craftsmen, Pete Grisel and Don Allen. Grisel was the metalsmithing expert and Allen the stockmaker. The idea was to craft fine rifles utilizing modern machinery and techniques while retaining the ability to provide many custom features unavailable from most factory operations. The first development of the duo was the flagship of the Dakota line, the Dakota 76 bolt action sporter. Utilizing the best features from both the pre-64 Winchester Model 70 and the Mauser Model 98, the 76 was styled cosmetically as a deadringer for the Model 70.

The rifle was an immediate success. Shortly after the rifle was introduced, Grisel left the company and Allen and his wife Norma took the helm. Since that time, two additional Dakota models have been introduced, the single shot Model 10 and most recently, the Dakota Legend double shotgun. It is a bit early to tell just how successful the shotgun will be, but the Model 10, last I heard, was outselling the Dakota 76. The first models of the Legend are limited production guns with exhibition quality wood and fully engraved. As a result, they are quite expensive. Allen will also be producing a couple other models of the gun that are not quite so fancy and will be priced

more moderately although still by no means inexpensive. Knowing him as I do, I would be willing to bet that his next new introduction will be a double rifle on the shotgun frame.

I have visited the Dakota facility in Sturgis, South Dakota, several times. It is a modern, well-equipped factory that employs around forty workers. The machinery is state-of-the-art computer-controlled equipment. The work force is comprised mostly of young and energetic craftsmen and women whose talents are just blossoming. Several of them could, most likely, make a living in the custom gun trade, however, most choose to stay with Dakota. I believe that says a lot for the company. While most of the work force is made up of males, it is also refreshing to note that many of the Dakota employees are women. All of the Dakota checkering is done by women and, I believe, the finishing as well. Women are also present throughout the plant and do many other tasks.

A quick look at its catalog will quickly emphasize why I call Dakota a semi-custom maker. The list of available options is almost limitless. Actually, there are thirty-seven options listed. A prospective customer can select the grade of the blank for the stock, buttplate desired, gripcap, bolt checkering or not, a stan-

192

The Dakota Model 10 single-shot rifle is now its best selling model. This one is the author's personal Model 10, chambered for the 7mm Dakota cartridge.

dard caliber or one of Dakota's proprietary cartridges, and on and on. The catalog lists three grades of English and three grades of Bastogne, in addition to the standard grades supplied at no extra cost. If in the Sturgis area, a visit to the plant is welcome and while there, the customer can personally select a particular stock blank from the many on hand. Only time and the depth of one's pocketbook limits what can be done. If a customer wants engraving, Dakota can arrange it. If the customer has a favorite engraver, he or she can arrange the engraving job personally and Dakota will accommodate those wishes as well. Ordering a Dakota rifle is almost the same as ordering a full-blown custom job without some of the cost, although electing many of the available options can run the tab up substantially.

A couple years ago, I had a hankering for one of Dakota's Model 10 rifles. I have been a sucker for single-shot rifles for as long as I can remember. I had long liked the Model 10, but it was a bit too diminutive for my tastes in its standard cartridge configuration. When Allen came out with his line of proprietary cartridges and slightly beefed up the Model 10 action to handle them, my will power vanished. I ordered one in the 7mm Dakota chambering. I had on hand a stock blank that I had saved for something special for more than twenty years. I also had a Heym stainless steel barrel already hammer forged for the 7mm bore. Heym makes or at least made exceptionally good barrels, but they were especially good in the 7mm bore. Finally, I had a new Leupold 2X7 variable scope in my goodie box. I bundled up all the items and shipped them to Sturgis. About six months later, my rifle was finished.

Allen had used the components that I provided in the crafting of my rifle. He sent the action, scope mounts, gripcap, and perhaps another item or two to

Doug Turnbull for his magical case coloring. The stainless steel barrel was farmed out to HS Precision for a coloring job. I don't know what process it uses, but the end result was most pleasing. I believe it uses some type of Teflon finish on stainless steel. Whatever it is, it works wonderfully. The remainder of the work was done in-house. The finished rifle is one of my prides. It is the epitome of what a single-shot rifle should be like, at least in my somewhat jaded opinion. Allen apparently also liked it because he used a photo of my rifle on one of his decorative tin plaques. It is a great rifle that shoots well and looks good.

Although Dakota Arms and its production is most familiar to me, it is not the only company doing similar work. Kimber started out producing top quality .22 rimfire rifles. It was very successful in doing so. As its success grew and its reputation soared, it branched out into larger caliber rifles and was in direct competition with Dakota. Its product lines were very similar. I have no idea what happened, but Kimber failed. Recently, Kimber is back on the market, but this time concentrating on its .22s and a few other products. As far as I know, Kimber is doing fine.

Another semi-custom firm is Cooper Arms. I'm not very familiar with its products, but it seems to be doing fine as well. There are a number of other firms that specialize in producing semi-custom products. Some, like Dakota, put out a high grade gun close to a full custom job. Others, like Ultra Light Arms, specialize in very lightweight hunting rifles. Still others, for instance, Kenny Jarrett, specialize in exceptionally accurate rifles. The list goes on and on.

Some custom makers also turn out a line of semi-custom guns. I remember reading that the late Monty Kennedy had such a line of rifles. I also know that Tucson custom maker Frank Wells also had a line of

193

Three Dakota Model 10 single-shot rifles. The middle rifle is still in-the-white, awaiting the customer's instructions for engraving. Photo courtesy of Dakota Arms.

semi-custom rifles at very reasonable prices. I don't believe that Frank still offers that service though, and is now concentrating only on full custom jobs. Whether any others are doing it or not, I can't say. Still, I'm sure there are some doing it.

Hopefully they will all do well in the marketplace as there is certainly a niche for the product. There are many shooters who are not happy with out-of-the-box factory models. Unfortunately, most simply can't afford a full-blown custom job from a good maker. Wanting is one thing, but making it happen is another. I would dearly love to have Dave Miller or John Bolliger make me one

of their fantastic custom rifles. If this book sells a million copies, I will plunk down an order for one from each. Until that happens, though, I guess I will just have to be content with what I have. My Dakota Model 10 will hold its own in most company and will do me fine. It wasn't crafted from muzzle to buttplate specifically for me by a single artisan—several had a hand in its making. Still, I had the ability to tailor the rifle to my wants. I'm most pleased with the results.

Chapter 15

The State of the Art Today

There is an old theory that laments the passing of the old guard in any endeavor. The prevailing tenet seems to be that once they are all gone, the quality of the craft, whatever it is, is doomed to mediocrity forever. This theme is particularly true in the gunmaking profession. I have heard it expressed about engravers, stockmakers, metalsmiths, and the entire British gun trade. At one time, I succumbed to the conviction myself. I moaned and groaned with the best of the naysayers.

Well, folks, I'm here to tell you that at least in the gunmaking profession, nothing could be further from the truth. That expectation, if anyone still subscribes to it, is absolute horsefeathers! I have seen the work of the legends in the custom gun field, at least a bunch of them. Many were good—very good. I have yet to see an example from any of them that comes close to the quality of much of the work being produced today. As I said in the beginning of the book, there are, I'm sure, many reasons for this fact. I am certain that lack of artistic talent and skills was rarely one of them. Even so, the quality of the work today far exceeds that of a few years ago.

It is difficult to find fault in most of the custom products available today. The more examples I see, the more mind boggling the quality becomes to me. Steve Heilmann's metalwork, for example, is as close to perfection as I have ever seen. Each time I look at one of his jobs, I think it can't be bettered. The next time I come across one, it is better, not by much, but better. This is true for all aspects of the gunmakers art as the same can be said of David Miller, Rick Stickley, Mark Cromwell, and many others.

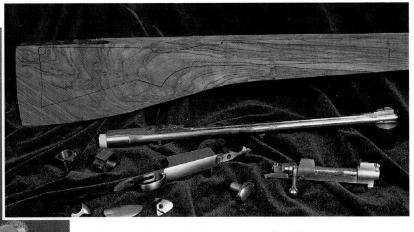

All the makings of a fine custom rifle: These components were crafted into the Grizzly Rifle by John Bolliger's Mountain Riflery. Photo courtesy of John Bolliger.

This custom Colt Single Action Flat-Top Model was custom crafted to re-create the famous target version. Original examples are very rare, so metal-smith Bob Snapp made one. Frank Hendricks did the engraving and Steven Dodd Hughes crafted the grips. Photo by Mustafa Bilal.

Engravers and their engravings are also good examples. For many years, I felt that very few American engravers were even close to their European counterparts in artistic talent in design and execution. To me, much of the work I saw was fairly crude. I saw engraved quail that looked more like a pregnant Gila monster than Mr. Bob. The scrollwork was often as ragged as my hunting shirt. Overall design was sometimes slipshod and the engraved scene as a whole just didn't mesh or flow. Naturally, there were exceptions, but most just didn't turn me on. It is far different today. There are any number of American engravers who can and do hold their own with anyone.

Checkering is another component of the art form that has been improved substantially, both in design and execution. Masters like Tom Shelhamer, Monty Kennedy, and Dale Goens (who is still making stocks at age eighty) did outstanding checkering. I didn't care all that much for Shelhamer's pattern design, but

his execution was superb. Both Kennedy and Goens were more versatile in design, I think, with equally precise execution. Even so, some of the work being done now is better. A checkering job from John Bolliger or Duane Wiebe is as good as it gets. Both turn out some pretty ornate and difficult patterns that are superbly done.

For many years, case coloring was a lost art. A lot of craftsmen and women tried their hands at it, but few succeeded. Most jobs stood out like a hooker at a church social. Doug Turnbull came along and changed that in a hurry—likewise with metal finishing. For years, there were two choices: rust blue and hot blue. These days, there are processes for finishing metal that would put an alchemist to shame. I don't claim to understand any of them, but they sure look good. How durable some of them are remains to be seen.

We have seen several ladies get involved in the business. I don't know of any that are custom 'smiths,

The SCI Leopard Rifle from the David Miller Co.: There can be no doubt that the finest custom work ever done anywhere in the world is being done right now in the USA.

An exquisite large caliber hunting rifle from the Tucson shop of Frank Wells: This rifle is intended to be used in the game fields of the world. Photo by Ron Dehn.

196

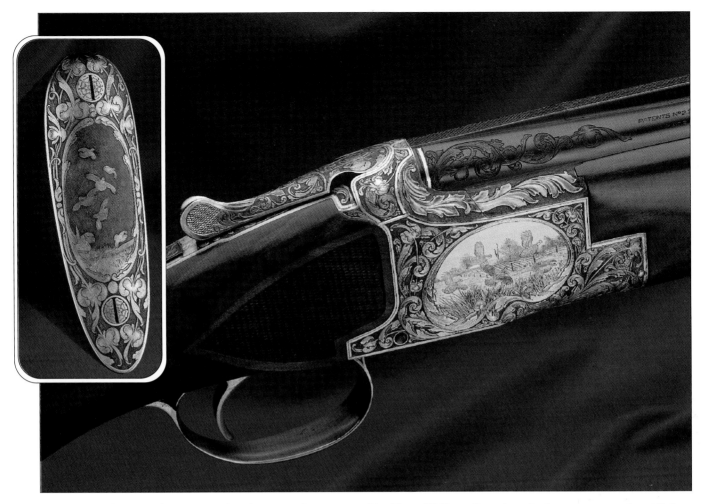

Two views of a magnificent Browning Superposed as engraved by Terry Wallace: Guns just don't get any more beautiful than this. Photo by Gary Bolster.

but I do know several who are heavily involved in specialties such as checkering, finishing, and engraving. Kathy Forster and Pat Taylor do great checkering. Lisa Tomlin turns out wonderfully delicate engraving patterns that are superbly done. I suspect we will see this trend continue.

I cannot think of a single aspect of building a custom gun that was done better in an earlier time. I believe that the finest custom firearms ever made are being crafted right now here in the US. Each year that passes sees improvements, often subtle, but still improvements. I don't think we have seen the best yet, for it is still to come.

Perhaps the single most promising aspect of the custom gun trade is the fact that many of today's best craftsmen and women are still quite young in years. I probably have shorts older than some of them. Even so, they are executing custom work that is scary it is so well done. Imagine how good they might be when they reach middle age.

I have heard for eons now that top quality walnut for stock blanks would soon be a thing of the past. The last of the trees were being cut and most of them

were being turned into veneer, the story went. Well, I don't have a census of walnut trees around the world, but plenty of excellent blanks seem to be available and new sources are turning up all the time. I won't say the supply is endless by any means, but there are obviously still plenty of good blanks available. Prices for good quality blanks continues to escalate. That is the bad news. The good news is that there doesn't seem to be any shortage of them on the market. True, exhibition quality blanks are rare, but then they always have been. Across the spectrum of grades, though, I believe that there are plenty still available.

Machinery and tools have been vastly improved over the years. Steel technology has been improved, walnut availability is at least holding its own and the technical and artistic skills of the makers has made quantum leaps. Added to all this, there seems to be a breed of client that is willing and able to pay the tab to justify the maker devoting the time it takes to do a spectacular job.

Even though still somewhat lacking compared to what it should be, the word is getting out as to just what is available out there in the custom gun field.

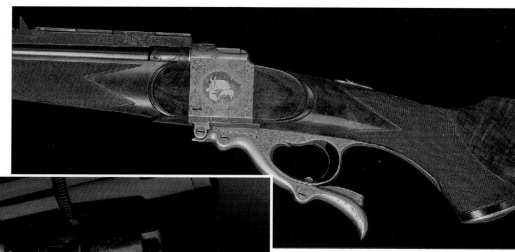

A Darwin Hensley stocked Farquharson single-shot rifle— Hensley has probably stocked more Farquharsons than anyone else alive. Photo courtesy of Darwin Hensley.

The combined talents of gunmaker Maurice Ottmar and engraver Terry Wallace created this magnificent single-shot rifle. Photo by Gary Bolster.

Not all custom rifles are large bore hunting rifles. Here are two .22 rimfire rifles that have had the custom treatment throughout. The top gun in both photos, a Winchester 1890 pump action, was stocked by Darwin Hensley and engraved by Bob Evans. The bottom gun is a semi-auto Model 63 .22 that was stocked by Jay McCament and also engraved by Bob Evans. Photos courtesy of the Firearms Engravers Guild of America.

The team of gunmaker Jay McCament and engraver Bob Evans produced this exquisite southwestern theme sporting rifle. To date, this team has produced four such southwestern theme rifles. Photo by Mustafa Bilal.

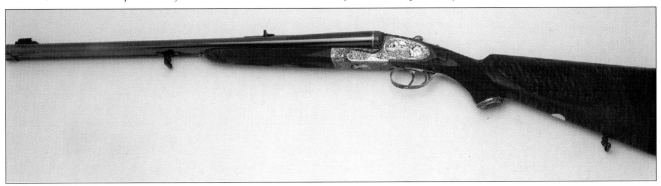

A magnificent Holland & Holland double rifle as engraved by Texan Ron Smith. The best quality London double rifle was an appropriate canvas for the artistry of Ron Smith. Photo courtesy of the Firearms Engravers Guild of America.

Few national publications have really covered the custom gun industry well. That is unfortunate. Perhaps the reason is that the custom guys and gals are not the best advertisers, I don't know. Perhaps I am wrong, but it seems to me from an admittedly faulty memory, that there is less custom gun coverage today in the national press than in the past. John Amber is gone, but his successor at the helm of Gun Digest, Ken Warner, continues to run custom gun coverage in his book. A few of the monthly magazines run an occasional piece on the custom trade. Most do it rarely, though.

I can understand the business of magazine publishing. It is well-known that advertising dollars makes or breaks any magazine. With that in mind, it is clear that magazines will primarily run material that will attract advertising dollars. Still, it would seem prudent for any magazine in the field to give some editorial coverage to custom guns. Most give precious little. There are a few, though, thank goodness, that give the trade excellent coverage. I believe that has helped immensely.

Finally, thanks to the efforts of the Guilds, the NRA, and the SCI in hosting their annual get-togethers, where enthusiasts gather and see what is going on. As a result, the word does get out. The makers have the opportunity to show the shooting public what they are capable of doing. They can talk to their potential clients and explain what their version of a custom gun is all about. After that, it is a matter of budget and time.

All these things together make the state of the art the best it has ever been and getting even better as time passes. For the custom gun aficionado, it is utopia, Noah's ark, and the Garden of Eden all rolled into one.

Chapter 16

Afterthoughts

I left myself some space in this chapter to ramble, philosophize, and blow a little steam—perhaps a lot of steam. I am, admittedly and unashamedly (is that a proper word?) a custom gun fan. I am also a devotee of the philosophy of the late Jack O'Connor. As such, I maintain that the .270 Winchester is about all the cartridge anyone needs. I believe that the pre-64 Model 70 Winchester is probably the best factory rifle ever built. I conclude that any custom rifle should be classic in design and form. I think that the big bore buffs are out of touch with reality and that the idea that a bore size of .33 with a 250 grain bullet is essential to take jackrabbits, is preposterous.

I begrudge little. If a particular sportsman or woman wants to use a .375 H&H magnum for his or her pet mule deer rifle, or a .458 Winchester for that

The author's pet custom rifle: It was built several years ago by the David Miller Co., but is totally different from its product today. This .270 has literally accompanied Turpin around the world. It will still shoot under .5 MOA any day of the week.

matter, that's fine with me. If, as I read from one authority (?) that he took his caribou with a .470 Nitro Express double rifle at 275 yards, amen. This same guru also recommended the .375 as a deer rifle while condemning the 7mm Remington magnum as a moose rifle. That's also OK by me. As far as I'm concerned, if a fellow wants to use a 105mm howitzer as a whitetail gun, that's fine. All I ask is that he let me know where he'll be hunting so that I can avoid the area.

Where I have a problem is when such a purveyor of infinite knowledge states that anything less than his recommended cannon is necessary for a particular game animal. I have hunted a lot with a .270. I don't have much experience with a lot of cartridges, but I have used a .270 enough to know what it will do. I don't believe that there is a better cartridge for game up to caribou size. I have also used a double rifle, including the .470 NE, a bit. I had just as soon throw rocks as I had shoot at an animal 275 yards away with such an elephant cartridge. I have taken several moose and been present when several others were taken. Mr. Moose has a glass jaw and hit fairly with a good bullet from almost any caliber, including the 7mm Remington magnum, results in a very dead moose. I believe a 100 pound Arizona Coues deer is more difficult to kill than a 1,500 pound moose.

My philosophy has always been "to each his own." So long as a caliber is at least adequate for a particular species, that's fine with me. If it is obviously overkill, that is equally fine. Often, confidence with one's rifle is every bit as important as the size of the hole in the barrel. Adequate bullet placement is, I think, almost always more important.

One argument that appears occasionally in print is that the .280 Remington is a vastly superior cartridge to the .270. The most often cited reason for this pronouncement is that there are more choices of bullet weights available for the .280. That is, of course, true; however, I have learned that it is impossible to kill an animal deader than dead! If there is an animal that can tell the difference in being fairly hit with a good .277-inch 130 grain bullet and a 140 grain .284-inch bullet, I have yet to see it.

One well-known authority wrote that the .280 was an inherently more accurate cartridge than the .270.

200

A very fine custom magazine rifle from the shop of Steve Heilmann. Heilmann does both metal and stockwork in his California shop. Photo courtesy of Steve Heilmann.

I asked several custom makers about this and was told that BS is BS. A couple makers I know won't even take an order for a .280 due to past problems in getting them to shoot accurately. I accept the fact that the .280 is a good cartridge and I even own a rifle in that chambering myself. Mine is more than acceptably accurate and a good rifle. It is, in my view at least, not one whit better than the .270. If a hunter wants to use the .280, so be it. Just don't tell me that it is better than the .270 on animals of appropriate size—that just ain't so.

I suggest that custom gun fanciers should have theirs built in whatever caliber they feel comfortable with and what has worked for them. Take your authorities with a grain of salt. I maintain that there is no substitute for experience and whatever one's experience tells him is right, usually is. It is difficult to argue with success. While I am the first to admit that a .270 is on the puny side for moose and would never recommend that caliber as ideal moose medicine, it will work. The only moose that I have ever seen literally knocked off its feet was hit with a .270. I have seen them shot with everything from a hot .300 magnum up to and including a .375 H&H. Typically, hit through the lungs with most anything, they will give little signs of being hit, wander off a couple hundred yards, and if not pushed, will simply lay down and die. It makes little difference what caliber was used.

If I had to recommend an ideal moose cartridge, it would probably be a .338 Winchester, .330 Dakota, or a .340 Weatherby. All will do the job nicely, but then so will several others. What does all this have to do with custom guns? Not much, except that if a hunter is hav-

ing a custom rifle built for moose hunting, that would be my recommendation.

While it is clear that my preference in custom rifles runs to classic styling, matte bluing, precise checkering in either a point or fleur-de-lis pattern, and a satin finish, that is my choice. If others like rollover combs, sharply hooked grips, white spacers at the butt and forend, fish scale carving instead of checkering, and gold inlaid maidens for engraving, that is their choice. None of us is right or wrong. What we choose is right for us, but perhaps wrong for many others.

Typically, we select a maker for our masterpiece based upon reputation, signature styling, the waiting list, and pricing. We select an engraver for the same reasons. These are all very valid selection criteria. Where some make a mistake is when the preferred maker has too long a waiting list or the prices are too high, and we go to another and request that he or she copy the preferred makers product. That is generally always a mistake. Most often, the resulting custom gun will be a disappointment.

There are many makers and engravers plying their trade. Surely one of them can meet the clients desires. Among the makers I know, it would be difficult to get one of them to build a rifle with nonclassic features. Most just wouldn't accept the job. I tend to associate with makers who turn out custom guns that are in line with my preferred styling. Even so, there are makers out there who prefer to do rollover comb stocks with white line spacers. There is, I am sure, a maker for all tastes in custom guns. Some may just be a bit more difficult to find.

A set of guns from Steve Heilmann: The double shotgun is of French origin, although it is every bit the quality equal of the London product. The rifle is a British-style express rifle. Both guns were metalsmithed and custom stocked by Heilmann, then engraved by Terry Wallace. Photo courtesy of Steve Heilmann.

This Winchester High Wall is from the shop of Steven Dodd Hughes. Custom guns today are not only modern bolt action rifles. Period pieces are also re-created, preserving our historical firearms. Not only are they re-created, but the new versions are far better than the originals. Photo by Steven Dodd Hughes.

Are custom guns worth their cost? The answer to that question must be answered with a politically correct response—yes and no. They are certainly worth their cost if the client is pleased. Hours and hours of very demanding and precise work does not come cheaply. Still, I don't know of a single maker who earns, per hour, what plumbers, auto mechanics, and electricians earn. Considered in that light, custom jobs are a bargain.

On the other hand, prices vary widely for very similar products. While one maker, primarily because of his reputation in the field, can command $2,000 or more for a custom stock, another might get only half that amount. There may very well be few differences in skill levels between the two. In that case, the latter represents a real bargain. Earning a reputation means paying one's dues and having done that, a known maker can demand and receive far more return for essentially the same work. This fact is true whether discussing custom makers, engravers, painters, or chefs.

As mentioned in Chapter 1, custom guns are generally not worth their cost if they are purchased as an investment. There are exceptions to that statement, but I believe it is mostly true. One exception might be that a client finds an up and coming maker early, has a few custom guns made by that maker, and later as the makers reputation and prices escalate drastically,

The author used a one-of-a-kind custom Heym .470 NE double rifle to take this stud dugga boy buffalo in Zimbabwe. Custom guns are for looking, but they are also for using.

The author used his pet David Miller Co. .270 Winchester in Africa as well. This record book warthog fell to a single shot from the rifle. Custom rifles are first and foremost hunting guns. Second, at least in my opinion, they can be collector pieces.

This Dakota Varmint model is the personal rifle of the owner, Don Allen. Chambered for the .22 PPC cartridge, it is super accurate. Though not an exhibition piece, it does yeoman duty at reducing the prairie dog population around Sturgis, South Dakota.

sells them at a substantial profit. I believe that rarely happens, though. Usually, clients have guns built to satisfy their desire to have it. Later, if for whatever reason, it is sold, it will typically realize about half what it cost.

The reason makes good common sense. If the cost approaches the price of having the builder make another, the buyer will most often have one built to suit him/herself. I was once asked by two friends of mine who were undergoing a divorce, to appraise my pal's custom rifles for the divorce settlement. That, I knew, was fraught with danger. Even so, I did it. The lady involved, previously a good friend, hasn't spoken to me since. She knew what he had paid for the rifles and when she saw my appraisal, she almost delivered a litter of horned toads! I'm sure she believes that her former husband and I conspired against her. I didn't, nor did he ask me to. I appraised them honestly and, I believe, fairly. My friend has similar tastes in rifles to mine. They were all very nicely done by reasonably well-known makers. One major problem when it comes to trying to market them though, was that he is a wildcat caliber fancier. Many of his rifles were chambered for odd-ball calibers. If there is anything more difficult to sell for a reasonable price than a custom rifle in a non-standard caliber, I don't know what it is.

Anyway, I would never recommend buying a custom gun as an investment. The odds are that a savings account at 2.5 percent interest would return more on the investment. Custom guns should be bought because the buyer wants them, and for no other reason. Either that, or, to satisfy some highly specialized requirement that is not available any other way.

I own and use custom guns because I am fascinated with them. I relish fancy walnut, precise workmanship, superb finishing, and most of all, I enjoy hunting. I cherish my custom jobs long after and before the hunt though. I get great satisfaction out of taking them out of the cabinet and rubbing on a drop of stock oil every now and then. I am pleased to show them to admiring friends and discuss their features. I also, once in awhile, down trophy elk and charging stud buffalo, right there in my den That's what the custom game is all about. They are made to be used and admired. I do both.

The quality of today's custom gun has never been better. The number of talented artisans crafting their products for the marketplace has never been higher. Their skill levels are, by and large, uniformly awe inspiring. There has never been a better time to place an order for a custom gun. Uncommon artistry is prevalent throughout the industry.

SOURCE DIRECTORY

ENGRAVERS:

John Barraclough, 55 Merit Park Drive, Gardena, CA 90247

Jim Blair, P.O. Box 64 - 59 Mesa Verde, Glenrock, WY 82637

Winston Churchill, RFD Box 29B, Proctorsville, VT 05153

Mike Dubber, P.O. Box 4365, Estes Park, CO 80517-4365

Bob Evans, 332 Vine Street, Oregon City, OR 97045

William Gamradt, 111 West Front, Missoula, MT 59802

Eric Gold, P.O. Box 1904, Flagstaff, AZ 86002

Barry Lee Hands, 26192 East Shore Rte., Bigfork, MT 59911

Frank Hendricks, HCO3 Box 434, Dripping Spring, TX 78620

Ralph Ingle, 112 Manchester Court, Centerville, GA 31028

Lynton McKenzie, 6940 N. Alvernon Way, Tucson, AZ 85718

Rex Pedersen, 2717 S.Pere Marquette Hwy., Ludington, MI 49431

Martin Rabeno, 92 Spook Hole Road, Ellenville, NY 12428

Roger Sampson, 430 North Grove, Mora, MN 55051

Bruce Shaw, P.O. Box 545, Pacific Grove, CA 93950

Ben Shostle, 1121 Burlington, Muncie, IN 47302

Ron Smith, 5869 Straley, Fort Worth, TX 78114

Robert Swartley, P.O. Box 3086, Napa, CA 94558

Terry Theis, P.O. Box 535, Fredricksburg, TX 78624

Lisa Tomlin, Rt 2, Box 263-B, Huddleston, VA 24104

Terry Wallace, 385 San Marino Ave., Vallejo, CA 94589

Ken Warren, P.O. Box 2842, Wenatchee, WA 98807-2842

Sam Welch, CSVR Box 2110, Moab, UT 84532

Claus Willig, Siedlerweg 17, 97422 Schweinfurt, Germany

THE SPECIALISTS:

Ted Blackburn, 351 West 900 North, Springville, UT 84663

Kathy Forster, 2124 SE Yamhill Street, Portland, OR 97214

Jim Hasson, 4425 E. Wildwood Dr., Phoenix, AZ 85044

Marvin Huey, P.O. Box 22456, Kansas City, MO 64113

Dave Talley, P.O. Box 821, Glenrock, WY 82637

Doug Turnbull, 6426 Co Rd 30 E Main St., Holcomb, NY 14469

Jim Wisner, 146 Curtis Hill Road, Chehalis, WA 98532

CUSTOM MAKERS:

Larry Amrine, 937 S. LaLuna Avenue, Ojai, CA 93023

Dietrich Apel, RR 2 Box 122 W. Brook Rd., W. Lebanon, NH 03784

Steve Billeb, 1101 North 7th Street, Burlington, IA 52601

John Bolliger, 1775 North Elk Road, Pocatello, ID 83204

James Corpe, 200 Holt Drive, Russell Springs, KY 42642

Mark Cromwell, RR 2 Box 122, W. Brook Rd., W. Lebanon, NH 03784

Gary Goudy, 263 Hedge Road, Menlo Park, CA 94025

Steve Heilmann, P.O. Box 657, Grass Valley, CA 95945

Darwin Hensley, 63133 E. Barlow Trail Rd., Brightwood, OR 97011

Keith Heppler, 540 Banyan Circle, Walnut Creek, CA 94598

Steven Dodd Hughes, 309 South H Street, Livingston, MT 59047

Jay McCament, 1730-134th Street Court South, Tacoma, WA 98444

David Miller Co., 3131 E. Greenlee Rd., Tucson, AZ 85716

Maurice Ottmar, Box 657 - 113 E. Fir, Coulee City, WA 99115

Bruce Russell, P.O. Box 697, Glenrock, WY 82637

Bill Simmen, RD 1, Box 210A, Vanderbilt, PA 15486

Bob Snapp, 6911 E. Washington Rd., Clare, MI 48617

Gary Stiles, RR3, Box 1605, Homer City, PA 15748

James Tucker, PO Box 525, Raymond, NH 03077

Ed Webber, Box 325 McLeod Road, Big Timber, MT 59011

Frank Wells, 7521 E. Fairmont Pl., Tucson, AZ 85715